I Will Never Forget You
The Rescue Movement in the Life of Joan Andrews

Joan Andrews in prison, 1988.

I Will Never Forget You

The Rescue Movement in the Life of Joan Andrews

by Joan Andrews
with John Cavanaugh-O'Keefe

IGNATIUS PRESS   SAN FRANCISCO

Cover design by Marcia Ryan
Cover photograph by Susan Andrews Brindle

CONTENTS

FOREWORD

When Ignatius Press called to ask me to write the foreword for this book about Joan Andrews, *I Will Never Forget You*, they related a story about Joan's current travels in England. Joan and twenty-five others were arrested for a rescue mission at an abortuary in Manchester, England, and they were facing a possible extended prison term. Then something strange happened.

A magistrate at Stockport Magistrates Court dropped all charges against them. Another prisoner, Maurice Lewis, had been jailed for five weeks at Strangeways Prison in Manchester for refusing to promise he would not rescue more babies at the South Manchester abortion center. Lewis' charges were dropped at the same time.

The basis for the magistrate's bold decision was his interpretation of the Act of 1361 that states that the peace must be kept for the Queen and all her liege and all her liege subjects. The magistrate reasoned that since abortion was illegal in 1361, the Act was intended to include peace for all of the Queen's subjects, including unborn children.

The Act of 1361 was read aloud in court, and all the prolife activists agreed to be bound over to keep the peace under the Act with the clear understanding that they would keep it for both mother and unborn child.

That the court officially interpreted the Act of 1361 as requiring the protection of unborn children is a testimonial that Joan and the other rescuers were simply doing a job for the Queen: protecting her unborn liege subjects. That has been Joan's preoccupation and consuming mission since she first learned about abortion: wherever she is, Joan is about the business of protecting defenseless unborn children.

Joan Andrews has been a hero of mine since her first extended incarceration for prolife activism in 1982, when she was jailed in St. Louis for contempt of court. Her crime was rescuing babies at a St. Louis abortion mill, in defiance of a court injunction protecting the abortuary from prolife direct action.

Joan and I did not meet until the early 1980s, but I sometimes wonder what would have happened to prolife activism if we had met when she first came to Chicago in 1973. Joan was not aware of my prolife work as Director of the Chicago Office for Pro-Life Publicity when she arrived in Chicago that year with a plan to enter an abortuary and disable the suction machine.

Joan's 1973 Chicago mission was aborted by a policeman who saw her on the street in the early hours of the morning. Since Joan could give the officer no reasonable explanation for her being there at that hour, he assumed she was a runaway. He put her on a Greyhound bus headed back to Tennessee, her plan to disable an abortion machine unfulfilled.

Had Joan and I met in 1973, the infant year of the prolife movement, we surely would have collaborated in a program of non-violent direct action. I imagine the first rescue operation would have been held in

1973, rather than in 1975. Joan would have wanted it, and when Joan has decided to embark on a course of action, it usually happens.

Because of her deep religious faith and prolife militancy, Joan is often called "Saint Joan of Newark". Saints are often two or three steps ahead of the rest of us, and they are often misunderstood. Many prolifers have misunderstood Joan's adherence to principles as simple stubbornness. Indeed, there were times during Joan's long months of solitary confinement when some of us thought she may have made mistakes in judgment.

I even wrote her a Dutch-uncle letter, urging her to get out of jail and come back to lead the troops. But her sacrifice in solitary confinement in a maximum-security prison in Florida galvanized the direct-action movement. She knew what she was doing, even though some of us did not see it as clearly as she did.

Joan could have escaped her prison ordeal simply by cooperating with the prison system. Judge William Anderson was willing to give her probation rather than incarceration. But Joan knew that cooperating was not God's plan for her life. She embarked on a policy of noncooperation and no compromise.

Although Joan is a hard-liner, she knows that each person's situation is unique. She would never criticize or look down on someone who, because of family or other obligations, would feel compelled to accept probation or pay a fine instead of going to jail. Joan is a person of deep and sincere humility. She once told a group of former abortionists, "You don't owe us an apology. We owe you one because we didn't try to convert you sooner."

What touches me most about Joan is her childlike simplicity. Jesus said, "Whosoever does not receive the kingdom of God like a little child shall not enter it" (Mark 10:15). Joan is that little child. She is highly intelligent and well-read, but she keeps a simple focus: abortion is murder, and we all have to intervene directly to save the babies.

When I visited Joan in prison in Delaware in April 1988, she radiated joy. We laughed and joked about things as if we were sitting in a pizza parlor. Joan, like the apostle Paul, had learned the secret of being content in any situation. "I give no thought to what lies behind but push on to what is ahead" (Philippians 4:13).

When I told Joan how much I admired her for what she was doing, accepting prison so joyfully, she replied, "What you're doing, Joe, traveling all over giving talks, would be harder for me to do than what I'm doing." I answered, "Well, if it's any consolation, I'll keep doing what I'm doing. I'm not ready to trade places with you." We laughed. Even after two years of solitary confinement, Joan never lost her sense of humor.

Our job as prolifers is to make the world see the victim, the unborn child. That is why what Joan has done is so beautiful. She became a victim herself and suffered severe hardship. After her release from prison in October 1988, reporters clamored to interview Joan. But before she gave any interviews, she insisted that the reporters view a short video tape, "Houston Proud?", a hard-hitting, graphic video showing aborted children. Some of the hard-boiled reporters were seen wiping away tears. They saw the tiny victims of abortion because they had come to interview another victim of abortion, Joan Andrews.

The formula for being a saint is simple. Ask, "Lord, what would you have me do?" And when you hear the answer, *do it*. Joan asked the Lord to show her his will for her life, and when she heard this answer, "Rescue those being led unjustly to death", she answered the call.

Joan is an inspiration to all of us who have heard the call to rescue the babies and wish to answer it. Her book, *I Will Never Forget You*, tells us how she did it. Let's hope we'll be able to follow her lead.

Joseph Scheidler
Chicago
August 1989

1 1960

Of course we rescue people who need us. We start to learn about rescues from our families.

In 1960, when I was twelve, there was a family picnic near the farm in Tennessee, and I was swimming with my cousins. There was a sandbar we could play on, right in front of where our parents were sitting. We were allowed to play there, but we were forbidden to go past a particular tree, because once we got past it, the water would be over our heads, and we could get swept into the rapids.

My cousin, Cindy Watts, went past the tree. She was only ten, but she was very adventuresome. She got into trouble, however, and started to call for help. I reached for her, but soon I was over my head, too. I kept trying to grab her, but I could not quite get her hand, and the current was behind my back, pushing me. She just kept slipping away.

When I looked around, my brothers John and Bill had run to get something. I did not know what they were doing, whether they were coming back or trying to get help or what. But right at that moment, they were not helping.

I was scared to death. I had been held under water once when I was younger, and drowning was the worst death I could imagine. I thought being shot would be

13

better. Two men had died in that same river the week before, down a little from where we were.

I was scared to go out there, but then I thought, "Oh, my gosh, I could not live if Cindy died." So I went after her. I was not a good swimmer. I could dog-paddle, but not much more than that. But I went after her as fast as I could, calling to her.

Below the sandbar and the tree, the river goes around a bend. As we went around that bend, the river swept us closer to one side. But we were still too far from the bank to grab anything. We were still some feet out from the right bank when I finally caught up with Cindy.

I went under her and tried to put her on my shoulders. We had reached another sandbar, so I could get my feet on the bottom, but the water was still over my head. I got her on my shoulders and started to walk in the direction of the bank. At that point, my brothers finally showed up with the log they had gone to get. With their help, we got out safely.

My mother was upset because the men were slow to respond, but she praised me for what I had done. She kept saying, "You saved Cindy's life! You saved Cindy's life!" and things like that.

That night when everyone went to bed, my mother took me aside and asked what had happened, what I was feeling when I went after Cindy. My mom was like that; she always wanted to know everything. So I told her that I had thought I was going to die. I knew about the two men who had died there the week before, swept away by the current. But more, I had thought, "How can I not go after her?" I could not choose to do nothing. Just watching was not an option. I had to go after her.

Cindy got married when she was in college, to a young man who had cancer. She knew he was dying of cancer. After he died, she got married again, to a man with several kids. Now she has several more and is the mother of a big family.

It was in 1960, on December 1, that we lost Joel. He was my youngest brother, two years younger than Miriam. We named him John Mary Joel, but we called him Joel. When we had learned my mother was pregnant, we had picked the name Joel for a boy. When he died, Mom wanted the names John and Mary also, for Saint John and the Blessed Mother. We know he was a boy. He was perfectly formed and alive when he was born, although he was premature.

We were all in school—including Daddy, who was the principal at Belfast Elementary School—when Mamma realized she was losing the baby. She called my dad and told him. He told us, and then he left immediately. John, Bill, Susan and I took the school bus home that afternoon. I remember it so clearly. It was awful. We walked home from where the bus dropped us in town, about four miles away. When we got home, Mamma was in the kitchen and the priest had already come out. Joel had already been born and died. Even though we did not see him alive, we were able to hold him.

The next day we buried Joel in a little cocoa can. (That may sound rather disrespectful since these days cocoa comes in cardboard boxes. Back then, however, cocoa came in beautiful silver boxes—probably aluminum, but it looked like silver—with little tops that you could pull open.) We pasted a cross on the can, a beautiful cross my grandfather had gotten in Europe. Then we each put in a lock of our hair, and then finally we put the little body in. We buried him on the farm. The priest had blessed a plot of land, and we had a regular funeral. We dug up two little cedar trees and planted one on each side of the grave, although they died right away because we planted them in frozen ground.

I remember walking around after that and thinking, "I'll never be happy again." I had never known a death in the family other than those of my grandfather and my uncle. But they were older, and although it was sad, it seemed all right.

We buried Joel next to a natural stone formation jutting up out of nowhere, near the pond. It is a pretty pond, with lots of trees. We would have preferred to bury him at the spring, which was the most beautiful part of the farm, but it floods there. We made a cement marker with a cross for him.

Since then, all the babies in the family who died before birth have been buried there. Susan's baby Christopher is buried there, and Miriam's two babies are there.

Before this, of course, I knew that when a woman was pregnant, she was pregnant with a baby. From the time I was little, I always wanted to get married, and I knew that if I got married I wanted to have lots and lots of kids.

When Mamma and Daddy stopped having kids, we thought that God should send some more. It did not seem that they were having as many kids as we thought they should be having or that God should be sending. We always knew it was in God's hands, but we still thought there should be more.

I must have been in fifth or sixth grade when a girl told me that some woman had had a baby out of wedlock. I said, "No way. God does not send babies unless you are married."

And she said, "No, this woman had a baby."

"No way", I insisted.

I knew babies were precious and knew they were from God, and I knew that a woman was pregnant *with a baby*. I never thought about how babies got started. It just seemed so natural when I saw a mother getting around. And then babies were just born. I just presumed it was a baby growing, and that was why the mother was getting bigger. I cannot remember a time when I did not think that when a woman was pregnant there was a baby growing inside. It was just so obvious. The woman is flat at first, and then she says, "I'm pregnant", and then she grows.

She grows, and so does the baby. Then a little kid is born, just a little tiny creature, and then it grows some more. It is just natural that the baby is all formed before birth.

Still, I was very awed when I saw how perfectly formed Joel was. He was just beautiful. He was so little, and every little finger, every little toe, was so perfect. He had a perfect little face. But we thought it was funny: he did not have any hair.

Bill and John, Susan and Joan.

2 Early Days

I was a coward when I was little. As a little kid, and even as a big kid, I would ask other people to buy things for me in stores, because I was shy. My mother did it for me when I was in elementary school. But even in high school, I did not like going into stores and talking to people. In fact, I hated school because I hated facing the teachers. I was scared to death of them. I was bossy with my sisters at home but too scared of strangers even to open my mouth.

I was almost always very respectful to my parents. One time I said something disrespectful about Daddy, and that scared me. It happened in 1952, during which Mamma had been in Europe for a whole year. My dad had taken us camping, and on the way back, we stopped at a mountain near Chattanooga from which we could see seven states. We saw some little kittens by the road and asked, "Oh, Daddy, can we take them?" And he said no. We were mad about it. Later, at home, Daddy made a tape recording of us, asking how we liked the camping trip. I said, "Oh, it was good."

He said, "Tell Mom about the camping trip."

I said, "Mamma, we found these little kittens, but Daddy would not let us take them home. Isn't he mean?" I said it jokingly, but then I thought, "Oh, my gosh!" I was ashamed that my mother was going to hear that remark. I was so remorseful. Mamma never spanked us, but I just did not want her to hear me say such a thing. I worried about it for another week, until she got home.

Of course, I was just four then. The point is, I was very respectful to my parents.

My mother's father had a big influence in my life. He was a gentle person, such a good person. My mom once told me that he had a real temper when he was young, but he conquered it. When I knew him, he was the gentlest person you could ever imagine. He would never whip us or scold us. If we ever argued, he would just pick up a cigar (although he had quit smoking) and put it in his mouth, and immediately we would stop fighting. We knew what he meant, even though he never explained it to us.

His name was Edward James Early. He grew up in Detroit, married Jessica O'Keefe, and had three kids. We called him Gampa, a name we made up, and we called our grandmother Ganger. He was shanty Irish; Ganger was more aristocratic Irish. She was related to Lady Sheridan Knowles, the "Blue Lady" in the famous painting. She told many stories about the family history. I loved them both very much, but Gampa went to daily Mass and seemed more interested in spiritual matters.

We lived in the small farming town of Lewisburg, Tennessee. I went to school in Belfast, which had a little combination post office and store, a feed store and a country school.

First, I went to a Catholic school, St. Catherine's in Columbia. That worked while Daddy was still farming, but when he started teaching, the driving was too much. Daddy drove us twenty miles to get there, then went on another fifteen miles to Santa Fe to teach. (They call it Santa "Fee". If you pronounce it Santa "Fay", they think you are an outsider.) When he was offered a job as principal of the school in Belfast, we all switched schools.

Once Susan and I ran away and tried to go back to the Catholic school, which would have been about twenty-seven miles from Belfast. Susan and I had planned it carefully. We had gotten enough clothes and food for a couple of weeks, put them in a bag and had a friend hide it for us. On the day we ran away, she gave us our bag and we took off.

We were gone for several hours. We ran away in the morning and hid in the woods, watching the cars drive by with people looking for us.

Susan started crying after just a couple of hours on the road. We were going to hide in somebody's barn and walk during the night, to make sure no one would find us. We were determined to get back to that Catholic school. But Susan said, "What will Mamma think? She will be worried." So we turned ourselves in.

We got to school, where Daddy was the principal. He was supposed to spank us. He knew our teacher would be listening right at his office door. But he was very understanding, and so he put us near the door and whipped his own hand with a paddle.

As each of us started high school, we moved to Nashville. Bill and John were first, and they were in a boarding house for one semester, but then my mom moved to Nashville and lived there in a house that my grandmother had. As each of us finished elementary

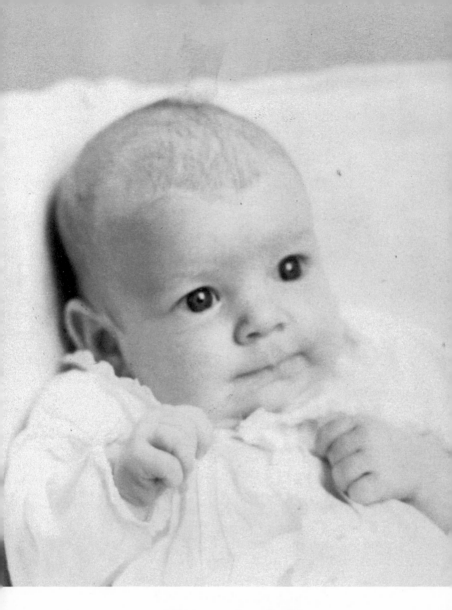

Joan, one month old.

school, we moved there too. When Miriam finished, Daddy got a teaching position in Nashville, and we all moved out.

I was at St. Bernard's for my first year of high school, and I tried to quit school a number of times. As soon as they let me off the bus at the school, I would walk home. It was just three or four miles. Eventually, in the middle of my first year in high school, they gave up on me and sent me back to the farm where Daddy was. I stayed with Daddy, because I felt so out of place in Nashville. I was from the country. I felt so shy, and these people were so smart.

I missed a semester of school and was afraid of starting again, so my parents decided that it would be easier for me to start at another school. I was scared to start at any school. I hated school. I really hated school.

But Mamma said, "Please, you must go to a Catholic school." And when the whole family moved up to Nashville, I had no choice.

In my second year, I went to Cathedral, and there were blacks there. I wondered why I had not found blacks at St. Bernard's, and I found out that the school would not allow them. It was just shocking. But it gave me a sense of pride about Cathedral, and I decided I wanted to stay there.

Some of the kids at Cathedral were involved in protests with their families. My classmates were going, and I wanted to go. But Nashville was very quiet. The protests were never violent as they were in other cities. In Tennessee, the blacks were very nonthreatening to the whites.

When I became a teenager, Daddy and I started

arguing about the Vietnam War. I would get upset, but he was always so controlled, just the way a person should be. When he argued, he would debate. I would always lose it and get upset.

I opposed the war, and I presumed that Susan felt the way I did. I do not really know, though; she never argued about it.

I started opposing the war in Vietnam in 1962, while I was still in high school in Nashville. No one else in the school thought much about it one way or another. I wrote papers on it and debated it with other kids. But I was too cowardly to debate it with teachers.

It was mainly my mom who got me interested in the Vietnam War. Of course, she did argue with Daddy about it. He really supported our U.S. presence there, and she had reservations. She was very critical of the monks who burned themselves. I thought they were sincere and believed in what they were doing. I knew there were Communist instigators who were using people, who assassinated their own people and pretended they were martyrs. But I felt the vast majority of the monks involved were sincere, even if they had been misled or duped.

I felt that Diem was a good man, that he probably would be the best leader you could get there. And if tiger cages were being used to hold political prisoners, which I was not sure I believed, I felt that we could use our power to get this stopped.

But our complicity in the murder of Diem and his brothers, Nhu and Can, was horrendous. Once that happened, when we tried to support the next government, it just got worse and worse.

When we started to send more than just arms—

started to send troops—that changed the argument. Mamma was pretty much against the war, and she was opposed to the way we were conducting it, which was totally immoral. Even if you support the cause, you still have to look at the way it was conducted.

In November or December of 1966, Billy, John and I heard a speaker at St. Louis University in defense of the war. But Bill and John found his talk so objectionable they started to change their view of the war. I did not change my position, but I did not like the disrespectful way the audience heckled the speaker.

In high school, I was the only one interested in the war. No one else even wanted to talk about it. So I was glad that when I got to college there was an antiwar group there. But some of the group members were very nasty in their attitudes. They had a deep anger.

Even though I treated my dad badly when I was angry, I would not call him names. I would argue and raise my voice and say bad things about the American flag. But I never called him names, never showed him disrespect on that level.

I always knew that the one side—the Jane Fondas and people like that—were blind to what the other side was doing, and I thought that was atrocious. That was the kind of thing I saw in the antiwar group on campus.

After one semester, I got fed up and quit the antiwar group. Maybe it would have been better to stay in the group and work for a change. That is what I would do in a prolife group now.

John got drafted that year, which was pretty much what he wanted. He had not filed to get a deferment while he was in college. He had decided that he would just go. When he got drafted, I felt really terrible about it.

The next year Bill volunteered, even though he had not yet finished college.

In the army, they both remained very antiwar. Still, John volunteered to go to Vietnam. It was never clear in my mind why he did that; I guess he just had to get away from where he was.

The army sent John to radar school, as they had promised when he joined, but then they put him in artillery. He told me at the time he just wanted to go over to Vietnam. But he said that if he was ordered to fire, he would refuse—that they would lock him up, or he would go AWOL, but he would not kill anybody. John was like that.

When Bill was drafted, he was supposed to go to Vietnam, too. He was sent to some swampy area in Louisiana to be trained for jungle warfare; he was going to be an infantryman. But when he got to Louisiana, the army needed clerks. He started working at Fort Belvoir in Virginia.

When John received orders to go to Vietnam around Christmas of 1968, Bill asked to go instead. If he had gotten orders to go to Vietnam, that would have kept John out. The army did not allow two brothers to serve at the same time in the war zone. He called somebody at the Pentagon, and his orders for Vietnam were prepared too. We did not know which was going to go. All we knew was that by Christmas, both had orders for Vietnam.

In the end, John was put on hold, and Bill went on over. John was then reassigned somewhere else, and he never went over there.

Bill was in Vietnam during the Tet offensive of 1969. (It was not the 1968 offensive but the smaller one the following year.) He saw horrible things there, and that was when he lost his faith. He did not think God could allow such evil.

At one point after I left college in 1969, I tried to get sent over to Vietnam, too. I wanted to go over as a nurse. I tried to get a guarantee from the Red Cross that if I were trained I would go to Vietnam. I checked out the army, too. But they were vague and would not offer any guarantee. So I discarded that idea.

In 1973, when *Roe vs. Wade* was decided, I was shocked. I felt that we had returned to the world of Nazi Germany. I had always figured that we lived in a civilized world, but now that had changed.

I remember that even as a child I was really horrified by the Nazis. I think I would say I was actually traumatized by learning about what they had done. That such brutality and slaughter could happen in a country that had been Christian, that we called Christian, was shocking.

Even in the 1950s, hearing about it scared me. When you are a kid, ten years seems like forever, so the Third Reich was like ancient history to me. But still I knew it was an event of modern times, not an event from the distant past, from the Dark Ages.

I used to try to imagine what it would be like to be a German living in Nazi Germany. How would I feel about my country?

So when I heard about *Roe vs. Wade*, I decided I had to do something.

It took me a few months of prayer and preparation to decide. I kept looking for the public outcry, but there was no outcry. People were not even marching in the streets. At Mass, the priests were not proclaiming that there was mass murder of children going on in this country, and we had to get out and stop it; that we had to go to these places where the killing centers were.

I expected to see action. But I did not see anybody organizing anything.

I was not organizing either. I figured I was just a twenty-five-year-old recluse; what could I do? And I will be totally honest: I was just the biggest coward in public.

I decided to go to Chicago to smash the abortion weapons. I chose Chicago because it was close enough to get to easily but far enough away so that my parents would not necessarily hear about what I was doing and be worried. But the idea just did not gel. I went there, but I did not do much. After a while, I went home.

In 1974, I worked with Ralph Schulz and the Tennessee Volunteers for Life, a prolife group that had started in Chattanooga and was trying to get chapters going in other places such as Nashville. (A parish priest put me in touch with Ralph when I asked if there was anything going on, anything I could do about abortion.)

We tried to get a chapter going in Nashville, but it was not easy. Ralph worked mostly among Catholics, and the early Tennessee Volunteers for Life were not really welcome in many churches. We tried to get literature in the churches, but even that was a struggle.

In 1975, we worked on the state legislature and got three bills passed, including an informed consent bill.

In one legislative battle, Susan testified about how she had been raped and become pregnant, and how the counselors at the "health" clinic had tried to force her to have an abortion. She testified about the pressure they put on her and the trauma when she lost the baby in miscarriage. She said she thought that the emotional trauma they caused her had contributed to the miscarriage.

We lost that one. Susan and the other two women who testified on behalf of the law were sued for $68,000 apiece by Planned Parenthood. The state did not want to fight it all the way, and they just paid Planned Parenthood. Susan tried to stop them from doing that, but did not succeed.

We worked in parishes in Memphis and Nashville, distributing literature. Ralph would give us a segment to look after.

Then Susan and I moved east, to Delaware. We had met some people in the Delaware Right to Life in 1974 when we were visiting there. When we went there, we picketed the abortion hospitals and abortion mills. We went back and forth for a while. In 1976, we were in Delaware full time, working with Delaware Right to Life. In 1978, we were back in Tennessee.

In June of 1978, we went with a group from Memphis to the National Right to Life convention in St. Louis. That was the first time I heard of a rescue. There was a flyer there about sit-ins at abortion clinics. I thought the National Right to Life convention was putting on the rescue and that all those hundreds of people attending were going to go out to the abortion mill and close it down. We signed up.

But Susan had been engaged for some time, and

her friends had organized a surprise shower for her in St. Louis during the time we were there. It was on Saturday morning, the morning of the rescue. Miriam and I were the only people in St. Louis from the family, so we thought we should go to the shower. We missed the action at the abortion mill. We had talked it over and had decided that we were not needed at the mill, since the whole convention was going. We wanted to be there, but decided we could just find out about it the next day.

On Sunday, we asked around, and no one at the convention knew anything about the rescue. Also, we had lost the flyer, and so we did not know whom to contact. It was as if the whole thing had just evaporated, evaporated into thin air. We figured it had been a one-time event. That was it. It evaporated, and we did not know where it was. We did not know there was a St. Louis group forming and doing rescues. We did not know anything about it.

There was a workshop on nonviolent direct action at the convention, but we did not see it. Some of the great leaders of the early days were there: Jeanne Miller, Lucy O'Keefe, Dave Gaetano, John Leary, Leszek Syski, Lynn Anne Szewczyk, John Cavanaugh-O'Keefe. But I probably would not have known what they were talking about if I had seen the title of the workshop in the program. We had just picked up a flyer, and then we lost it.

In those days, so many people got involved that way. They picked up a flyer at the March for Life and got all excited. Sometimes the flyers ended up in the hands of those who were just waiting for something like this, knew it was great and wondered why they had not been doing that before.

But we lost our flyer, and then the convention ended. We went back to Memphis and then eventually back to Delaware.

In the spring of 1979, three babies were starved to death at the hospital in Wilmington. The nurse who broke the story was threatened and had to keep her name secret. So we started picketing the hospital. All summer, we picketed every day. I walked to and from Wilmington, about thirteen miles.

We put up flyers about help for women facing unplanned pregnancies (unplanned by them, of course—from God's perspective, no pregnancy is unplanned and no child is unwanted). We put them up in restrooms in Newark and in restrooms along the highway from Newark all the way into Wilmington. In Wilmington, we put them up in the restrooms in all the public or semipublic buildings, in offices and restaurants, everywhere. Women who needed help would call us. Some were not pregnant, but many were.

The flyers were pretty simple. "Pregnant? Need help? Call Susan or Joan." And then they had our phone number. They said we would help with a place to stay, or whatever women needed. The flyers were all pretty basic: "Choose life; don't get an abortion", with little tear-off tags with the number to call.

When we were getting ready to leave Delaware, we had two women staying with us. One woman already had several little children. The other woman wasn't pregnant. She had been living with an older man, and he had been beating her up. She called our number and said she was not pregnant but needed help, and she needed it immediately; she had to get out that night. She said she had already left the house and was afraid to go back. She told us where she was; we picked her up and so she stayed with us. Before we left Delaware, we got her into another home, and we also got the mother with her children set up in appropriate housing.

3 The St. Louis Campaign

In his recent encyclical, Sollicitudo Rei Socialis, *Pope John Paul II said that abortion is a social sin and that the way we gain our freedom from massive social evils is by acting in solidarity with the victims of injustice. That response should come from a community, as well as from individuals. Building community response has been a long struggle.*

In 1978 and 1979, Mary Ann Kreitzer and Dave Gaetano worked to encourage the religious leaders of northern Virginia to lead a community response to abortion. The net result of their effort was a small march led by Bishop Thomas J. Welsh. The night before his march, an abortion clinic across the river in Maryland was torched (prolifers are still convinced that it was an inside job, especially since the abortionist's medical records were found in the trash a block away). Media coverage of the arson overshadowed the bishop's march and effectively deterred any action more forceful than marching.

In 1979 and 1980, Samuel Lee worked to build a community response in St. Louis. He won the support of many religious and civic leaders. Police in St. Louis County arrested rescuers but hired a plane to advertise pregnancy aid services during the rescue. Judges listened to the necessity defense and accepted it. Beginning in Lent of 1980, two people offered them-selves in place of the two victims of abortion every time an abortionist's enticements lured a woman toward his door. Even the abortionist was affected; for a period of time, he was discussing his childhood faith with a priest. But that community response was broken by Archbishop John May, who stood in front of the abor-tion mill and ordered people to cease the activity that was offensive to the community—by which he meant rescues, not killing babies. The campaign sputtered out.

Harry Hand and other leaders of the Prolife Non-violent Action Project worked to build a community response in Maryland, beginning with a large rescue in May 1984. One hundred and forty people, risking arrest, closed an abortion mill in Gaithersburg. There were no deaths; there was no exploitation that day— and only a few arrests. The campaign lasted through the summer and into the fall. In November, during a rescue in Wheaton, forty-seven rescuers were arrested, including seventeen clergy. It was reasonable to expect that the clergy would be back, with congregations. But again, nonviolence was overshadowed by arson; the site was bombed two days after the rescue. Clergy sup-port ended abruptly.

Beginning in 1984, Pennsylvania activists built a strong network of activists who prayed together, pick-eted together, coordinated sidewalk counseling and carried out rescues. Working with prolife politicians, they had some success closing mills. The year 1984 was also when concerted efforts to change prolife meet-ings began. At the National Right to Life convention in Kansas City that year, about one person in ten left the halls of the convention and went into the streets to protect children. All of the abortion mills in the city closed rather than risk confrontation. Since then, rescuers have been determined that, whenever prolifers gather in large numbers, that gathering will make a difference to babies; it will include some protective action. The March for Life, the annual National Right to Life conventions and the symposia sponsored by Human Life International have been obvious occasions for rescues. At three of the last five national conventions, the cities where prolifers met were abortion free for a short period of time. Similarly, at three of the last five marches in Washington, the city has been abortion free (or close to it—abortions may have continued in hospitals and doctors' offices).

But the rescues during prolife meetings were not the actions of a community. People came from across the country to help for a few days in some other community. The number of local rescuers was a relatively small portion of the whole.

During the "We Will Stand Up" campaign to make the papal tour abortion free, seven of the nine cities that Pope John Paul II visited were abortion free while he was there. But again, the work was done by a national coalition pulled together by Juli Loesch, not by local communities. The rescues helped to encourage local action, especially in New Orleans, but the activity during those two weeks was national.

Randy Terry's great work in organizing Operation Rescue was the spark for many strong local rescue groups. Operation Rescue's focus on New York and then Atlanta pulled people from around the country into those cities. Once there, they received excellent

*training, which they took home. And the list of cities
that had rescues in October 1988 showed clearly that
strong community action had become possible.*

*In 1989, Rex Moses pulled hundreds of churches
together in Austin, Texas, for a real community response to the killing. Rescuers there announced that
there would be no killing in any of the city's three
abortion mills from February 11 to 18.*

*When abortionists are confronted with an aroused
community that is determined, by God's grace, to protect children, what can they do? Abortionists can still
find allies among judges and legislators, in the media
and among the rich. Besides the criminal prosecutions
of rescuers, there will be more and more lawsuits. But
in the end, regardless of the chaotic state of the laws
on the books, a community that is determined to protect
children can do so.*

—jcok

After the failure in Northern Virginia, the second serious effort to organize a broad-based community response to abortion was in St. Louis.

Rescues first came to St. Louis in 1977. Vince Petersen started organizing in late 1977, and the first rescue was at Bolivar Escobedo's mill in Manchester in
January 1978. There was a good group of people who
risked arrest, including people from St. Louis University and St. Bonaventure Friary. But no one was arrested. The police did not want to make any arrests,
and the mill shut for the day.

The first arrests in St. Louis were in March 1978.
Six people were arrested, with thirty to forty more

people there supporting the rescue. Many of them were from Missouri Citizens for Life.

That case came to trial in November 1978, and they were convicted by a jury. They appealed and got a new trial (*trial de novo*) in the summer of 1979. At that trial, they were acquitted on the basis of the necessity defense.

There were several more rescues during 1979, at Reproductive Health Services in St. Louis and at Ladies Center in University City. There were two large rescues (large by the standards of that time) in the fall of 1979, in September and November.

The St. Louis team worked hard to organize their rescues. When they arrived at a mill, they knew what they were doing. They had their counselors lined up. In the picket line they had musicians who kept everyone praying and ensured that the spirit of the work remained prayerful. They had a good number of picketers. They got to the mills on time. (Once, in 1976 in Washington, some rescuers went into a mill after the abortions had started. They were so shocked by that, by the added danger to the mothers, that rescuers never made that mistake again. Now rescuers always get inside the mill, or get to the door, before the killing starts.)

There was a good legal team, with David Danis and Jerry Murphy, later joined by David Drury and Andrew Puzder. There were many others, but these four took charge.

The rescuers were a very democratic group, with meetings to talk about all the issues that came up. Of course, when they started having rescues every week, there were fewer meetings. Besides planning what

they would do, they also made careful critiques of
what they had done.

One long debate was about how to treat police. At
one rescue, someone called them Nazis. Was that fair,
or were the police victims, too? That issue was never
completely resolved, although people made a tactical
decision that it was bad public relations to be filmed
calling police Nazis. With that decision, all the
philosophizing was set aside. It is funny how many
decisions are made that way, based on accidental details, not on the real issue.

The St. Louis people got acquitted over and over,
in the city and in the county. They were acquitted on
technical questions, when the police could not identify
people properly, and on the more substantive question
of the necessity defense. In fact, the necessity defense
worked well until 1983, when it was taken to an ap-
peals court. The rescuers took a calculated risk, trying
to get a court of record to recognize the defense. They
let a case go by, let a lower court convict some rescuers,
so that they could appeal to a higher court. But they
lost. And after that decision—in *City of St. Louis vs.
Klocker*—they could not successfully use the necessity
defense in lower courts anymore.

Vince Petersen started PEACE (People Expressing an
Active Concern for Everyone) of St. Louis, with
Samuel Lee. Later, Samuel Lee came to the fore, and
Vince stepped back a little bit. By the time I got involved, Samuel Lee was the leader. That was in 1979,
when Miriam went to St. Louis to attend nursing
school and bumped into the rescue movement there.

Miriam started nursing school at St. Joseph's in

Philadelphia but then decided to switch to St. Louis. Soon after arriving, she heard that there would be a meeting about rescues there. After the meeting, she called Susan and me in Delaware and said she had found the rescue movement again in St. Louis—that they did rescues and that there was a rescue group on campus called PEACE.

We asked her to tell us everything she had learned about how to do rescues, and we would organize them in Wilmington. From the moment we heard of it, we knew it was the thing to do. What could be better? It was just the natural response to defend babies right away.

Miriam told us that what you do is find out how many execution rooms are in a killing center. Then you have to have one person to block each room. Susan went into the abortion mill in Wilmington and found that there were three killing rooms, so we knew we had to recruit at least three people for the rescue.

After trying for a while, with little success, to get people together in Delaware, Susan and I decided to go to St. Louis and get some experience so that the people who were following us would feel that we knew what we were doing. So we moved to St. Louis.

Our training was pretty slow. We went there, and nothing happened. No rescue was scheduled. Miriam had started nursing school in September, and had gotten involved in the rescue movement then. But when Susan and I came down in October to do a rescue mission, all we did was go to meetings.

Around that time, Dave Gaetano and the Prolife Nonviolent Action Project were distributing a manual on organizing rescues, and the opening line in the

manual was "Call a meeting". I would rather eat
spinach all day. But anyway, we had a meeting and
saw some role playing. The St. Louis leaders were
talking about scheduling a rescue, but then they decided to put it off temporarily. Eventually they did
one, in November, but by then Susan and I had already
gone back to Delaware, where we had our own rescue
scheduled.

But for all our efforts, the rescue fell apart in the
final week. People kept dropping out. The last straw
was a couple of days before the rescue was scheduled,
when we were down to just three people willing to
risk arrest, Susan and I and one other person. Then
the spiritual advisor of our third rescuer advised him
against participating.

When he decided not to join us, that left just Susan
and me. And since the Wilmington Women's Health
Organization killing center had three killing rooms,
or "procedure rooms", we thought we had to have at
least three people, at least one person at each door.
We were also not sure that both of us should be inside.
We thought that perhaps Susan should stay outside
to counsel the women as they came in.

We thought that having at least three people to
block doors was the only possible scenario. We did not
realize we could just block the outside door, or just go
in the waiting room and start telling the truth about
the place, or just take responsibility for one mother
and child and just stay with them, or do just about
anything we wanted to do. We were rigidly committed
to one scenario. That was my excuse, anyway. So we
dropped from the original seven people planning to
rescue to none.

After that resounding vote of no confidence, we decided to pull up stakes and move to St. Louis, not just for some training, but to stay and do rescues there. We had a pregnant girl staying with us, and it took us several weeks to get her and her child situated elsewhere, in another home. But when we had taken care of her, in mid-December, we were ready to move.

We spent Christmas with our parents. Then right after Christmas, on December 26 or 27, we made the big move. We went to St. Louis and got an apartment there. Miriam moved in with us. We were ready, just waiting for the next rescue. We waited and waited, then waited some more. We rushed down there the day after Christmas, and we waited until March.

Susan had been planning to be a part of the rescue movement in St. Louis, but she got married before the first rescue. She had been dating Dave Brindle for about four years, and on January 22, they got engaged. They were married in March, and she moved back to Delaware. Miriam and I stayed in St. Louis.

Samuel Lee was talking to religious leaders all over the city, trying to get support. He talked to the police, explaining what the rescuers would do. He spent some time trying to develop a relationship with the abortionists and their staffs. He talked to reporters to make sure they understood who he was and what we were planning. He was working hard. But we were waiting.

Samuel did not ever lay down the law or order people around; we discussed everything. But in the end, we arrived at a decision to start rescues on March 8. And after March 8, there were rescues weekly for months.

Prior to that, all the rescues had been planned in

David and Susan Brindle and children.

secret. People would sneak into the building and hide in the washrooms. Then they would sneak around until they ended up inside the abortuary—in the killing room or the waiting room—and then block doors. But this time we announced our plans to the public, including where we were going and when and how and why.

We had over one hundred picketers, far more than we had ever had before at an abortuary. And we had a lot more people who were prepared to risk arrest. Before that, the largest rescue they had organized in St. Louis was twelve people, at the November rescue that we had missed, and that had been considered a large group. So when we got over thirty people ready to do a rescue, just by announcing it openly, that was impressive. Maybe all that talk, all those meetings throughout the area and all those stories about it in the papers had helped. I don't know—maybe if we had continued to have rescues, they would have grown naturally. But anyway, it was big.

Samuel had said he wanted to build a campaign of civil disobedience with broad community support, and he had done it. From the first day, we had good numbers of rescuers and even better numbers of supporters. It was just a start, but it was big.

That first day was hectic. When we arrived at Escobedo's abortuary in Manchester, police were all over the parking lot. Then the picketers arrived and swarmed all over the property. At first, everybody went everywhere, and the police did not know who might be risking arrest, who was counseling, who was picketing or who was just watching. There were people marching and singing right through the whole building, going in one door and out the other. The police did not want to arrest us, and they did not know how to arrest so many of us.

All of us who were going to do the rescue walked onto the parking lot. At first, we could not get in the front door because security guards and police were blocking it. But we started to crawl under their legs, between their legs, all around them like ants, and we got in. That did not go on very long; they just gave up and let everyone in. So the rescue team went right through the door.

The building is like a mini-mall. It has a lot of open space, big enough to drive cars through, with potted trees and irregular angles to give the illusion that you are walking through a garden near some buildings, although you are really inside a building. Well, we took over that fake garden. We had a large group milling around inside the building, plus sidewalk counselors and a couple of picketers who also came in. It was a scene.

At that time, there was only one abortion mill in the building—Bolivar Escobedo's mill. Since then, two others have moved out there—Reproductive Health Services and Roitman & Palmer.

When the first woman tried to get in, a whole group of us blocked the door, but the police dragged her in, right over us. Then they dragged a couple of our people away.

It was interesting to see who was there blocking the door. During those months, we were always being put down, especially by teachers on the St. Louis University campus, as a bunch of college kids from the sixties, when in fact we had people of all ages and backgrounds. Barb and Jim Howard, for example, were established and respectable people. Jim had his own business. That day, respectable people were trying to stop the holocaust. Barb was dragged down the hall, and Jim was left by the door. The police struggled to gain control of the door, dragging people in over us and then trying to shut the door to keep us out. They pulled Jim away from the door and threw him on the floor.

That was when I got my finger broken. After the officer pulled the mother into the abortion mill and knocked Jim out of the way, he tried to push the door closed. I was next to the hinge, and I had accidentally put my fingers in the crack for leverage to keep it open. He threw his whole weight against the door, because something was jamming it, although he could not see clearly what the "something" was. Of course, it was my fingers.

At first I was in too much pain to scream. I could not even make a noise. But someone realized what was happening and told the officer, and he stopped immediately.

The police wanted to take me to the hospital, but I refused to go unless they agreed to bring me back. They would not do that. Fortunately, someone else said he would follow us to the hospital and bring me back, so I agreed to leave. I got my finger bandaged up and came back later in the day.

When I was first taken away from the door, my hand was bleeding, and someone announced, "The police did that!" For a moment, there was a great deal of anger there. And of course the police had just helped a mother get into the mill. I responded as quickly as

I could, saying, "No, no, it was an accident", and I tried to explain what had happened. I think the captain really appreciated that, because later he was very careful about the way I was handled. The officers said, "Now, why don't you walk away, we don't want to hurt you", and things like that. They were very solicitous.

After that, Samuel was determined that the whole action would be orderly, and he started imposing order. He ordered everyone out. "All picketers out to the front. All sidewalk counselors out, except two to stay in the main building." Of course, the police could not get any of us out, but people obeyed Samuel pretty well.

He put one counselor in each wing of the building, watching the two main doors where people might enter. Except for the rescuers and the counselors, he wanted everybody out.

The rescuers stayed in two groups, one group by each door of the abortuary. Inside the building, in the twisting corridor, there were half a dozen different offices.

The building had two main doors, and inside the building the abortion mill had two doors. We had the rescuers, a group of fifteen to thirty people, praying constantly off to one side. Two at a time, they blocked each door. The police did not do anything about the rescuers sitting in front of the door until someone who wanted to get in came along. It was much quieter then.

By the time I got back from the hospital, things were very orderly. No one was charging the door, and the police were not tossing anybody in the air. I blocked the door again, later that same day. I was one of the last ones arrested that day.

Some weeks later, incidentally, the police captain's son was with the prolifers, risking arrest to protect women and children. During a rescue, while some of our people were blocking the door, I overheard the captain say to an officer, "Listen, my son is going to block the door, and I don't want to arrest him. Will you do it?" His son was home from college for the summer. But it was already late in the abortionist's schedule, and no more women or couples approached the door that day, so he never did get arrested.

Months later, around the end of the summer, at the abortion mill in University City, I saw the captain again. He had come out there just to observe. We had not seen him for a while. I went up to him and asked, "Did your son ever get arrested?"

He looked at me, shocked, and asked, "What do you know about that?" When I told him how I had overheard him, he explained that no one else had come in that day, and his son never did get arrested.

That day, Samuel decided to announce openly that the next rescue would be on the next Saturday, at the same place. After that, the open announcements became standard.

The main abortion mill we targeted then was Escobedo's in Manchester. We went back to the same place every week, with a large number of rescuers. But sometimes one or two of us—Jeannie Klocker and I or someone—broke off from the main group and went to other mills. That was when I learned that you could do a one-person rescue. Jeannie and I started one Saturday when the rescue group was at Manchester with large numbers. We went into the city and did a rescue at Reproductive Health Services (RHS). After that, I went alone sometimes, or sometimes with just a few people.

We never split up the whole group, having half of the people go here and half go there, or having smaller groups go to several places at the same time. The main group kept going to Manchester. But a handful of us who were going off privately to do rescues elsewhere did so with the approval of the leadership.

Samuel Lee, who was leading the rescuers, is a Catholic. He had taken over leadership after Vince Petersen got things started; Vince also was a Catholic, a seminarian in a Franciscan community. Our principal law student (later rescue-lawyer), Tim Finnegan, was Catholic also. And the majority of rescuers were Catholic. But the 1980 campaign was not exclusively Catholic.

Shortly after the campaign started, a new group of people came for the first time—Evangelical Christians, mostly from a Presbyterian seminary, Covenant Theological, that was associated with Francis Schaeffer. They had seen *Whatever Happened to the Human Race*, and they became very involved. Those seminarians came down week after week, as picketers; they became a real force.

One Saturday in Manchester, I was with the first wave arrested. We were all in the big glass holding tank at the county jail in Clayton, when all of a sudden we saw another load of rescuers being brought in and unloaded from one of the paddy wagons, with eight or ten handcuffed Evangelical seminarians. It was their first arrest. We screamed and clapped!

They had been talking about it, and we knew they were pondering it and praying about it. But all of a sudden they finally did it, and they did it in a group. They were the last ones arrested that day; most of the regulars were already in the holding tank. When they saw that the door of the abortion mill was unprotected, they went ahead and acted. It was great!

The campaign seemed to be growing. At least at the abortion mill in Manchester, two people were arrested every time a woman or couple approached the door. More and more people were getting involved. We were saving lives pretty regularly. The community was fairly supportive. Even the police were supportive, hiring an airplane to fly over the abortion mill when there was a rescue, Saturday after Saturday, towing a banner with the Birthright telephone number or a prolife message. The police also organized a beef-and-beer fundraiser for the legal defense fund.

Most important, there were at least a couple of officers who refused to go to the abortion mill. One was a sergeant who would head to the farthest end of his district whenever he got a call about trespassers at the abortion mill. He simply would not respond to it.

Police support eroded over time, when there was an injunction, and we moved to another mill and when Archbishop May told them that they were bound to enforce the law. Probably the real prolifers, the strong ones who lived their commitment to truth and charity when it came to such questions, continued to do what they had to do—defend life or do it no harm.

The situation facing a police officer at an abortion mill is very difficult. There are arguments about whether rescuers should block the doors, but you do not have to agree that they should do it to understand that once they do, some things have changed. Once prolifers block the door, babies are safe and women are safe. Nobody will die there, and no women will be exploited, unless the abortionist can get his operation moving again. He needs help before he can kill. If he cannot find some muscle to clear his door, he cannot kill. If he hired bouncers to keep his door open, everybody would understand clearly that the bouncers were a part of the abortion machine, necessary parts of the killing industry. But they do not hire their own bouncers; they just call the police.

When the police find rescuers blocking a door, they have a very serious decision to make. They know that as long as the rescuers are in the door, everybody is safe, and nobody will be killed. They know that if they remove the rescuers, there will shortly be a pile of corpses inside. It is a stark, clear choice: remove the rescuers and babies die, or leave the rescuers and babies live.

But the police are ordered to move the rescuers. They feel that they have to enforce the law, regardless of the consequences. Although this generation grew up with a horror of the Nazi era, completely aware of the grave dangers of blind obedience, most police officers still decide to obey the order to remove us.

Of course, any police officer who decides that he will not obey blindly is risking his job, his career. The rescuers at that time were not risking much, just a few days in jail. For the police to follow their consciences may be far more costly. So we cannot judge them harshly. We should offer them support when they take risks.

Unfortunately, the Catholics on the police force got very bad leadership. Archbishop John May, shortly after he was installed as the archbishop of St. Louis, came out to Manchester to discourage us. He came right out to the parking lot, and then he went into the building. He talked with Samuel Lee and other rescue leaders, with the police and with the media. His visit was on the news. He was interviewed on television, standing in front of an abortion mill, criticizing what he found to be a serious problem. The problem he saw was not that some doctor who had been raised as a Catholic was killing babies. No, the problem that the archbishop wanted to clear up was the trespass that was going on. He told us we should not be blocking doors, that we should only be on the sidewalk picketing, not "breaking the law".

That was very interesting, because at the time he made this statement we had never been convicted in a court of law. He was presuming our guilt in the eyes of the law before we had ever been convicted of any wrongdoing.

All over the country, prolifers had been arrested blocking access to abortion mills or blocking the doors of the killing rooms. And they all said that they were not guilty of trespass because they were there to save lives. In our legal tradition, common law follows common sense, and it is just common sense that you can trespass, or even break and enter, to save a life. In fact, you can smash down the door of someone's home to save mere property, such as a painting threatened by a fire.

If you see a child drowning in a swimming pool, but the pool is surrounded by stern warnings against trespass, you can ignore those signs to save the child.

And you do not have to be afraid that you will be arrested for trespass.

In our law, that is called the "necessity defense". Sure, you broke the letter of some statute, but it was necessary to do so to protect a higher good, to save a life.

The question at an abortion mill is whether there is such an emergency as a drowning child. The abortionist does not think there is any emergency, but he is not the one who is on trial. We are on trial, and we say we had good reason to trespass. So we have a right to explain our rationale, and unless the prosecution can prove that there is no basis for our reasoning, then we should be found not guilty.

Even in the disastrous *Roe vs. Wade* decision, the Supreme Court dodged this question. They declared that the state would be neutral, would not try to decide whether an unborn child was a member of the human family. Having declared neutrality, they said that the government could not prosecute the abortionist.

If they are neutral, though, they cannot prosecute us for protecting babies. To set aside the necessity defense, they have to take a firm stand, not a neutral stand, and say that there is no rational basis for our belief that unborn children are precious human beings.

In two states, Virginia and Missouri, judges had listened to that argument and agreed with us. So in Missouri, nobody could say that we were breaking the law. Our lawyers pointed that out to the archbishop, but it did not seem to make any difference to him. The courts said we were not breaking the law, but he said we were. He never made a retraction or apologized. In fact, he went on to publish articles criticizing what we were doing, calling it "ill advised and counterproductive".

It was so painful to be there, watching him. There were picketers out there, and that was fine with him; they were doing what they were supposed to do. But there were also sidewalk counselors talking to women, and we were blocking the doors. The archbishop told us to leave this last line of defense of the babies, to remove ourselves!

It was so bizarre to see him at an abortion mill, at the site of the slaughter, but to understand that he was not there on behalf of the direct rescue of babies.

The leaders who spoke with him told us later about the things he said. Basically, he was there to tell us to stop blocking the door, but his whole approach was disheartening. He would talk only about the "issue" of abortion, about public relations and turning people off and breaking the law and all this technical stuff, when little babies were about to be torn apart. He was standing right there at the door to hell, where thousands of babies had died and thousands more would die, and he was there on a day when killing was scheduled.

There are many people who argue about the "issue", but never go near an abortion mill. Then, when they actually see the place, they are very shaken by it. It is one thing to argue about when life begins or some other interesting philosophical question. It is another thing to stand at a door and see women approach, knowing that if they go in, there will be a dead baby there in an hour or so. The cold reality is very different from the late-night argument. But there was the archbishop, at the site of the killing, making all the silly arguments that you would expect to hear in a college dorm. It was indeed bizarre; it seemed very unreal.

We immediately lost a great deal of our support. We lost almost all of our picketers. They thought they would be disobeying the bishop by even supporting a rescue mission.

Many of the experienced rescuers were firm in their commitment to protect children and women, but after that point, we did not get any new recruits. The short period of phenomenal growth was over; we came to a standstill.

After the archbishop, however, the campaign continued, though it was not as strong as it should have been. Then the injunctions killed it off.

We had been so effective that the abortionist Bolivar Escobedo had begun asking to see different prolifers, just to talk to them. The first person he asked to talk with was Jane Gibson. She was afraid to go into the abortion mill alone, so a young man went with her. They talked for about an hour.

There was a woman waiting for her abortion, and the nurse kept coming in and saying, "Dr. Escobedo, you gotta do this", and he kept saying, "Wait, wait one minute." They talked for almost an hour, closing that abortion mill for almost an hour. Finally the nurse insisted that he had to abort the child, that the woman was all prepared. Then Escobedo asked Jane if she would wait for him.

She couldn't believe it: "What? What? Wait here while you go in and kill a baby and come back? You're crazy. I'm going to block the door! I'm not going to let you do that!"

Escobedo asked if they could talk later. Eventually, Jane left his office, but she stopped in the waiting room on her way out, where she started counseling women.

The police, who were already there, told her to leave. She refused, so they arrested her. But as they were taking her out, Escobedo intervened on her behalf, saying that he had invited her in. So they dropped that arrest. It was a wild scene.

Escobedo also asked to see a priest. In fact, he asked to see Father Danis, one of the two priests who had been getting arrested with us. Father went in there with him for about half an hour. When he came out, he said what they spoke about was confidential but that we should pray very hard, because Escobedo was on the brink of making a decision.

Father James Danis was the brother of one of our lawyers, Dave. It was a real family affair; the lawyer's wife, Nancy, was also a rescuer. It was actually because he and Father Stephen Bauer got arrested that Archbishop May decided he had to break things up. Father Edwin Arentsen, just by coincidence, was arrested by himself across the river in Illinois on March 8, the same day that the campaign in St. Louis started.

Father Danis and Father Bauer stopped only when they received direct orders to stop. Then they continued to come out and support us until they were ordered to stop that also.

Father Danis died the next year. A brain tumor showed up about six months after he was banned from doing rescues. He hung on until fall, then died in November 1981.

But in 1980, after Father Danis saw Escobedo, we

were all very hopeful. Escobedo was definitely thinking about quitting; he let us know that. His business
was way down. It had come down from about forty
babies being killed on a Saturday to five even getting
into the abortion mill. The rest of his scheduled patients just did not show up, or they were rescued at
the door. We saved four or five each week.

We were able to keep track of many of them, because they went to a crisis pregnancy center, and we
followed them through birth. The rescues were very
effective, and Escobedo was going out of business.
Further, he was really stirred by what he saw. He
called himself a Catholic, and his kids were in Catholic school.

But then the injunction came down, and we were
all ordered to stay away from that mill. After a long
debate, the ill-fated tactical decision was made to move
on to another mill. Since then, Escobedo has opened
two more abortion mills.

In the debate over the injunction, the rescuers and
the attorneys all met together. Some argued that we
did not have to break the injunction right away or
challenge it immediately. We could just go to another
abortion mill. Babies somewhere else were just as precious as babies dying in Manchester.

The hard-core rescuers did not want to move to
another mill. They argued that we were committed to
the babies in Manchester. They argued that in all the
time since we made a commitment to protect babies
at that mill, we had not left. And we had a commitment
to this abortionist. We were there for him too, and he
was about to turn away from death. So how could we
abandon them and go elsewhere? Babies all over the

world were being killed, and all of them were precious. But we were committed to these.

The only thing that had changed, argued the hard-core group, was the injunction. If we left, that would be saying that we would not save babies as we had planned because of a piece of paper. If the only reason that we were not saving babies there was because of that piece of paper, that would give tremendous credence to it. Among those who said that we should not move on were Loretta Wagner, Ann O'Brien, John Ryan, Miriam and I, and we argued with the lawyers all through the meeting that night.

I was very proud of Loretta Wagner. She really fought for staying. Then she pressed to see whether we were all supposed to agree to move on or whether it was optional.

The lawyers gave their big pitch. They argued that we could rescue babies for free now, so why should anybody end up in jail, where they would not be able to rescue? For the time being, rescues were free, and we could all go to the next abortion mill; we could all go to University City. If that closed down, we could go to St. Louis. When rescues were enjoined, we could go to Bridgeton. We would all move together as each injunction came down, and when the final abortion mill got an injunction, then we would all break the injunction together. And the lawyers said they would join us. That was the big pitch.

Some of us were never convinced by the argument. It seemed that we were just giving credence to something that merited none and that we were going to cut our own throats eventually. But I did believe that we would all break the injunction together when the time came. I had a lot of confidence in those good people.

I thought it was bad to let judges think that we were afraid of the injunction, to let them think we were afraid of it when we really were not.

The lawyers said we could save more babies elsewhere before we had to go to jail. And of course we were novices. But it seemed to me it was just common sense that if we backed down at first, then the judges would think they had some power. Then if we challenged that power later on, they would have to save face.

If we broke the injunction right along with the trespassing laws and everything else, if we totally ignored it, then we would give the impression that we had not done anything new. But once we built it up so big and obeyed it, then the judge had to save face and hit us hard. We had already shown him that we believed that the injunction was a big thing and that when we broke it, we knew we were doing something really grave.

Although some of us just absolutely said no, the lawyers' proposal sounded good to many people. We put it to a vote, with an understanding that the majority vote would rule. The lawyers' proposal won, and, reluctantly, the hard core went along with it.

I felt then that we were making a bad mistake. And of course, as it came about, no one broke the injunction for a long time. A couple of years later, just four of us broke it.

So after the injunction in Manchester, the group moved to University City. That was when we started going out to the mill during the week. The killings were scheduled on two days there, Wednesdays and Saturdays. We went every day they were killing.

A few of us, including Ann O'Brien and myself, had already been enjoined from rescues at University City by early summer. We had been photographed there and ordered to stay away. We wanted to break the injunction, but we were persuaded not to. The argument was that if we broke the injunction, when just a few of us were in jeopardy, then the courts would hit us hard for it, and the harsh penalty that we received would discourage everyone else and scare them off when they were named in some future injunction. The leaders of the group said that we would have to wait and all break the injunction together.

Ann and I said that the few of us who had been enjoined should go to another abortion mill and rescue there. But again, the leadership said no, you can't do that, because then the abortionists will get an injunction for that place before the big group comes. So we were just boxed in, with the majority of the lawyers and everyone else saying, no, you can't do that, you're going to hurt the movement.

Ann and I were told by prolifers not to do any rescues in St. Louis, not anywhere in St. Louis. We were told that if we did, we would hurt the movement. So we picketed and counseled, and that was all we did that summer, until finally that mill got an injunction covering everybody.

Around the same time, Reproductive Health Services in the city also got an injunction. A few people had occasionally done rescues there, without telling the lawyers. But that place was enjoined, and we were told, "Don't touch that place."

By the summer of 1980, there were injunctions at Escobedo's in Manchester, at Ladies Center in University City and at RHS in the city. The only mill left, then, was Roitman & Palmer in Bridgeton. So of course we said, "Let's all go to Bridgeton."

In Bridgeton, the abortionists quickly stopped doing abortions on Saturdays. They still killed on Wednesdays, which had been a day when a large rescue group had been able to get out in University City. The abortionists sought an injunction but never got it, because they were clumsy in court.

But their failure did not make any difference, because the rescue movement was paralyzed by then, almost dead. After the third injunction, rescues died out, and no one was willing to go out except Ann O'Brien, Samuel Lee, John Ryan, Laura Armstrong (later Dunn), Mike Reid, Miriam and me and occasionally someone else.

We continued to do rescues in Bridgeton, and that was when we built up our long rap sheets. The judge there, Judge Harold Johnson, just would not hear our cases. What he said out loud was, "I dismiss this case." In effect, he said a little more: "Keep up the good work." So we had a free hand. We would go only during the week, because Saturdays there were not killing days.

It was a very good summer. Prolifers were working with so many pregnant teenagers that we could not find places for all of them to stay! At that time there were about twenty women and girls who needed a place to stay. We did not have our maternity home then, only the archdiocesan home. So we started working on a home that eventually became Our Lady's Inn.

In our apartment, we offered hospitality to one girl who came to us from a social worker named Miss Jones, who worked with pregnant teens, and then we had two more women who were turned away from the abortion mills by sidewalk counselors while we were blocking doors.

Susan, Miriam and I had gotten this apartment, for three. Then Susan got married and left, and we were able to offer the space to pregnant girls. Then we had lots of people in there. Janie Gibson had some problems with devil worship going on in her dorm, so she ended up staying with us, too.

We had the pregnant girls toward the end of the summer, but they did not get along with each other, so Pam Bizaillion took one of them into her apartment. Pam was a social worker, with a master's degree in social work. She was involved in starting Our Lady's Inn. Miriam and Jane and I helped to look for possible buildings to use and other similar chores, but Pam really knew how to go about it, how to get a business to back her, how to put together a payroll, how to get a lawyer to do all this for them. We went around with her and learned a lot.

Pam is the one who finally set up Our Lady's Inn and became its director. I was a staff member until I had to resign because of a misunderstanding.

A big argument was about whether we would have to take in anybody that needed a place to stay. There were some people who did not want to take in any underage girls, because we could get in all kinds of trouble for that. But we said, "No, no, everybody. We don't have to have the sanction of the state. We're going to take in people who need a place to stay. That was the format of the people who originally started this."

Another struggle for the board of directors was about doing rescues. The home started as a rescuers' maternity home, and rescuers were going to run it and rescuers were going to continue to rescue. But then, as more and more money came in, people started getting very cautious, and the board decided a person could not rescue and still be a staff member. The bylaws contradicted the principles of the people who set the place up.

There were some pregnant girls that stayed at Our Lady's Inn who were ready to join us at the mills. Some came out to the rescues while they were still pregnant, and others came after their babies were born. They did some sidewalk counseling, and some actually blocked doors. But as the Inn developed, they were told they could not do that. These were mothers who had been going to have abortions themselves, whom we had taken right from the abortion mill, and some of them wanted to go back and do sidewalk counseling. But it turned out that they could not do that, because most of the board members were against rescues.

The members of the board were really great people, but after Archbishop May came out with his position, they deferred to him, not in agreement, but out of expediency for the home. I do not mean to be critical of those good people. There were rescuers who made these decisions. But if we are going to avoid the same problems in the future, we have to be honest about what happened when there were problems.

For me, Samuel Lee was an enigma. He did prolife

work in reverse order. He started doing rescues, and now he is doing things that I used to do but gave up on. Everyone else I know started doing rescues after trying all this other stuff and finding out that it did not work.

It was not just Samuel, though. There were other people who did some rescues and then, when we got a maternity home, said, "That's the way we should go, maternity homes all over the country. No one will kill a baby out of desperation because they don't have a place to stay! We don't have to do rescues!"

It was mind boggling to me when I saw people taking that stance. Of course, we have to provide support for pregnant women, but that is not the heart of the issue. People kill babies for lots of reasons. Very few do so because they don't have a place to stay, very, very few.

You cannot stop the killing just by offering help. And you can't limit your work to people who want to have their babies but are in a little temporary financial trouble. We have to help people who do not want to have their babies, regardless.

When people say, "No, thank you, I'm going to kill my baby anyway", we still have to rescue them and their babies. We are not there just for people who stop and realize that we are right and remember that they really love their babies. We are there also for people who ignore the sidewalk counselors. For them, we block the doors, and say, "No, you can't do it."

Despite all our successes, the rescue movement died. I do not understand how this happened. A large group of rescuers moved from Manchester to University City. We had a large group there doing rescues on Wednesdays. In Bridgeton, the judge was allowing us to do it without penalty. But almost everybody gave up. I just don't understand how that happened.

Samuel Lee says that people just got worn out. The same people were getting arrested week after week, going to court—and trying to raise families and pay bills. The big problem was that we were not able to recruit new people.

While Miriam and I were working with the people in Maryland and Philadelphia, she met John Lademan and eventually moved back to Philadelphia to be closer to him. Then I moved back to the East Coast, Laura got married and started having babies and Ann worked during the week, so she couldn't do weekday rescues unless it was a real occasion. So John Ryan went out to the Bridgeton killing center all by himself. Often, he got beaten up by the police. They would arrest him, although he was never prosecuted. That went on for several years, until we finally decided to break the University City injunction, hoping there might still be some part of the rescue movement in St. Louis ready to do that.

4 First Arrest

My first arrest was in Manchester, Missouri, near St. Louis, at Bolivar Escobedo's abortion mill. The police were very gentle with me because I had a broken finger.

Before you are arrested, you usually get several warnings, from the police and from the owner of the mill. Sometimes you get whisked away in just a minute or two, but usually it is a very elaborate process, with repeated warnings.

At that rescue, I was handcuffed when they got me to the paddy wagon, not when they first arrested me at the door of the mill. But most of the time they cuff you as soon as you are placed under arrest.

There are steel handcuffs and some new plastic flexicuffs. When the police use steel cuffs, you can usually avoid having them cut into your wrists too much by flexing the muscles in your hands when the cuffs go on. That does not make the cuffs so loose that you can take them off, but it does give you a little extra room so the cuffs don't keep you in pain on the way to the police station.

The flexicuffs are generally used for large groups. They are similar to the plastic strips that you see in the grocery store holding bunches of vegetables, but they are stronger. Flexicuffs are a little nasty. Metal

cuffs have one loop to hold your right wrist, one loop
to hold your left wrist and a chain to hold them together. But the flexicuffs do all three jobs at once. So
they are always either too loose, so that you can take
them off, or too tight, so that they cut your wrists.
Guess which choice the arresting officer makes.

Metal cuffs can be adjusted, but flexicuffs can only
be tightened. If they are too tight, they can be cut off
and replaced, but that is a waste of money. Once you
have them on, you will probably wear them all the
way to the police station.

After you are handcuffed, the police usually take a
picture of you with your arresting officer to identify
you in court. The photographer sometimes asks you
to smile. Prolifers are nice people, and they usually
smile when they are asked to. But in this case, you
are being removed so that babies can be smashed.
Smiling may not be appropriate.

Next, you are loaded into the paddy wagon, or police
van. Some of them have a partition down the middle,
so that the police can put men on one side and women
on the other. Sometimes they use separate wagons
for men and women. Sometimes they put everyone in
together, figuring that prolifers probably will not harm
each other.

In the wagon, there is often a tremendous sense of
relief. The struggle is over, and you did what you could
do and did not chicken out. But that sense of relief is
always mixed with a clear understanding that once
the rescuers are gone, the babies die.

From the time you are arrested through the time
in jail, Scripture takes on new meaning. All kinds of
things that you might have read before without much

special interest suddenly have great significance. Getting arrested for saving lives is probably the best Scripture course available in the country.

The singing in paddy wagons is often very good. The sound is similar to singing in a shower; you have flat walls all around, sending the sounds right back to your ear. Of course, the quality of the music is not just because of the walls; it is also good because you are with prayerful people who want to praise the Lord.

At the station, the police take off your handcuffs, take all your property and put you in a cell. When they are taking your property, they often take your shoelaces. I had not expected that when I was first arrested; I did not know what to expect. The idea is that you should not have anything that you can use to kill yourself, so you have to walk around in floppy shoes.

The police take people out of the cell one at a time for processing, which includes fingerprinting, mug shots and floods of paperwork. The fingerprinting takes some time, since each finger is done on each of several records. The mug shots, one view from the front and one from the side, just like the pictures in the post office, are pretty quick. But the paperwork is incredible. It goes on and on, as the police fill out one form after another. They have to do all the writing themselves, asking you for the information. After watching some poor guy tapping out your name on an old typewriter or writing it laboriously by hand on form after form for an hour, you begin to understand why they worked so hard to persuade you not to stay in the doorway at the mill. They were not just being nice to you; they really did not want to spend the rest of the day on paperwork.

For many people, the worst part of the whole experience is the boredom at jail, waiting and waiting. The company is good, but the setting is drab.

Sometimes we are put in cells by ourselves, away from the rest of the prisoners. But more often, we are mixed in with everyone else. There is not any reason to be afraid of that, though. Most people in jail hate abortion and like prolifers. Also, they usually respond to people who care about and listen to them. Simple human kindness is in short supply in jail, and people respond to it. Also, of course, prolifers liven the place up with stories and singing. Prolifers are a good sideshow in a dull world.

The shared prayer, the music and the stories can be very uplifting. The first time I was arrested, I was very excited about it. But now, I usually just go to sleep.

After processing you, the police have to figure out whether they will hold you or release you. At my first arrest, I was released late that afternoon.

Generally, prolifers will not let their friends feel abandoned at such a time, and you will see people from the support group when you get out.

5 Cancer

In the summer of 1979, cancer started growing in my right eye. I had no knowledge of it. Usually this type of cancer metastasizes and spreads to the liver or lungs. Later, after you die from it, an autopsy reveals that it originated in the eye. Very few people find it in the eye first.

In October, while we were in St. Louis waiting to do a rescue there because we wanted some experience before our Delaware rescue in November, I went home to Tennessee to sell a horse. I got kicked, and I fainted and landed on my head. A doctor later told me that the cancer had evidently been growing for six months and the concussion caused it to detach from the retina. I started having signs right after that. The next day, I had some numbness on my face and loss of vision. The loss of vision continued for the next six months or so, so that by April of 1980, after the rescue campaign had already started in St. Louis, I was blind in that eye. Then I finally saw a doctor, and that was when I learned that I had cancer.

When I told the optometrist my symptoms—that I had been going blind since October, and I was sure it was because the horse kicked me and the concussion of the blow detached my retina—he asked me why I took so long to come in. I said that I figured it wasn't serious and so I had time, and I wanted to save money. I was doing rescues then, and I told him about the rescues in St. Louis.

I told him that I did not have much money, but that I had finally decided I could spare twenty dollars, which would probably be enough just to get checked out.

He did it for free. But he said, "I think you should see an ophthalmologist at a hospital." He might have said, "You need to see somebody right away", but he said it in such a low-key way that I never dreamed it was cancer, never dreamed it was life threatening. So I waited another month.

At the end of May I finally went to the hospital. That very day, they told me I had cancer. It was already throughout my lens. They suspected it was malignant melanoma and started running some tests.

I saw the doctor on a Thursday, and he wanted to admit me right away. I asked him if I could go in on a Saturday afternoon or Sunday, since it was so close to the weekend and we had a rescue scheduled, and he finally agreed.

He told me I had cancer, and he told me what the risk was, but I pointed out to him that it was not as imminent for me as for the babies. I told him I was not careless with my health. I would have come to him much sooner if I had suspected it was cancer or anything like that rather than just a detached retina. I thought a detached retina could just be reattached, and it certainly is not life threatening.

Still, at that point, since babies were scheduled to be killed the next day, I knew that if my cancer had been going on this long, it could wait until Sunday.

And so I said, "I'll go right in on Sunday." And I did.

They operated on Wednesday. The cancer had not spread outside my eye into my brain, so they just removed my eye.

My brother John had just flown in from Saudi Arabia and happened to be in Tennessee when he heard about the surgery, and he came straight to St. Louis, and my parents drove up. Miriam was already with me. Bill and Claudia came up from Columbia, Tennessee, to be with me in the hospital.

I was scheduled to get out on Saturday after the operation. But I asked the doctor if I could get out on Friday, and he said okay. So I was able to go back to the abortion mill on Saturday, and I was very glad of that.

When the abortionists in University City got an injunction soon after that, they did not have any trouble identifying me because I had a big patch on my eye. Also, they said, I was all over the parking lot.

My eye doctor was in the same complex of medical offices as the University City abortion mill. I saw him before any of the rescues there, while we were still in Manchester. But about two weeks later we started doing rescues in University City, and then shortly after that I was enjoined from the whole complex. I was enjoined from going to see my doctor because the abortion mill was at the end of that complex.

The doctors at the hospital were telling me they thought I only had a couple of months to live because they thought my cancer had probably metastasized. They ran tests to find out, and it turned out that it had not metastasized.

The doctor also said that the cancer could recur, especially if I were under stress. But I am always happy, and I didn't feel I had that much stress. I thought if I sat at home while babies were dying, I would be under much more stress.

The funniest thing was, we had a girl staying with us then, and she had a great big dog at one point. He had an eye infection, with all this yellow stuff coming out of his eye, and he had some eye medicine that looked just like mine. When I came home from the hospital I was using stuff in my eye, but later I realized that it was the dog's medicine.

6 Jailed in Baltimore

While we were living in Delaware, we worked with the Philadelphia activists, and we also joined the Maryland activists in many of their actions. The first time I went to jail was in Baltimore for a rescue at Planned Parenthood on Howard Street, near Baltimore's bus station. The rescue—or sit-in, as we called it then—was on August 8, 1981. It was one of the rescues that people were doing all over the country to mark the Feast of Franz Jägerstatter, which is actually on August 9. But that year, August 9 was a Sunday, so the rescues were on the previous day. This was the fourth year that prolifers observed this anniversary of the death of Franz Jägerstatter.

Jägerstatter was an Austrian farmer who refused to cooperate in any way with the Nazi war machine in his country. When he was ordered to report for induction into Hitler's army, he reported but refused to take the required oath. After some months in jail, he was beheaded in Berlin, on August 9, 1943.

Jägerstatter had been a regular, easygoing person until he encountered the abortion controversy. He fathered a child out of wedlock, and that really changed his life. He left his hometown for a couple of years, and when he came back, he was changed. He had become very devout and was scrupulous about

taking responsibility for his own actions. So he denounced abortion, and he denounced Nazism.

The things he wrote two generations ago about abortion would sound familiar to prolifers today. He said
abortion in Austria was worse than what Herod did,
and he compared abortion casualties to war casualties,
showing that abortion had taken far more lives than
all of Austria's wars.

He asked for advice from his pastor and even his
bishop, and they urged him to bend a little, to be a
good husband and a good father and not to stick his
neck out. But because of his views on personal responsibility, he refused to let the Nazis dictate to him. He
took it very seriously. The Nazis could not put up with
that kind of resistance, so they chopped off his head.

We were in Baltimore, trying to imitate Jägerstatter's courageous stance against brutality and com-
placency. Nine of us got arrested there that day.

When we went into the mill, Marilyn Szewczyk was
very calmly talking to the security guard. He was all
excited, but we just ignored his orders and went to
the killing rooms in the back of the mill.

In the back hallway, where the killing rooms were,
we locked arms two by two in front of each door and
started singing and praying. We could not see the
pregnant women from there; they were in a waiting
room, where our counselors were talking to them.
Larry Hamm was also in the waiting room, sitting
quietly and not doing anything to reveal that he was a
prolifer. After the police arrived and started taking us
out, he heard one woman ask, "Why are they arresting
those people for singing?" That gives you an idea of
how terrifying our presence was for the women there.

We were back there singing, and I was blocking the door with Maggie Gunther, who was doing her first rescue. She had done a lot of writing, encouraging rescues, but this was her first arrest. She was there as calm as she could be, and just so full of peace, and I was shaking like a leaf. I was trembling all over. I remember thinking, Hmm, this is interesting. I tried to stop myself from trembling all over, but I could not stop.

John Ryan, after some four hundred arrests, still trembles, madly so. The time beginning with the night before a rescue is tense. You hope that you will get there, that you will be able to do some good, that you will not be totally thwarted before you get into the killing room. There is always a lot of tension there, and it is very hard.

When the police dragged us out, it hurt; it really hurt. The handcuffs cut into my wrists that time. They were using steel cuffs, not the awful plasticuffs that they use when they are dealing with large numbers, but the cuffs were too tight anyway, and I was in pain. On the way out, they dropped me. I do not know whether it was an accident or whether they just decided to drop me. But of course, when your hands are cuffed behind your back, you cannot protect yourself when you are dropped. Then they dragged me down the long hallway and threw me in the paddy wagon.

The trial came up in just a few weeks. It was a complete farce. The judge did not even try to pretend that what happened in his courtroom had anything to do with justice. He was another one of those judges with a Catholic background who have always been some of our worst enemies, beginning with William

Brennan. Religion is supposed to pervade a Catholic's entire life, and so when a Catholic tries to "set his religion aside", it is impossible to predict what will be left.

The Prolife Nonviolent Action Project published the whole transcript of that trial, but I am embarrassed to read it. I did not do very well on the stand. When I was explaining why we went inside—to save lives and for the sake of the parents of the unborn children and the abortion staff and the whole community—the judge interrupted and asked, "If the doctor was about to perform this abortion, what were you going to do? Take the knife away from him?"

I started to explain that we try to get there before it gets that far, but he interrupted, "Answer my hypothetical."

I said, "Well, if I tried to take the knife away, there might have been a struggle, so I would not do that. I would not try to struggle with anybody."

Then he asked sarcastically, "What would you do in the operating room, just stand there and scream, or what?"

I kept trying to talk about using my body as a shield, but he did not buy it. Later, I thought about that question for a long time.

In the end, he convicted us and imposed stiff fines. Some of the people there had family responsibilities or other conflicts, and they decided to pay. Leszek Syski had been in the first group of prolifers who went to jail for refusing to pay a fine, in Connecticut in 1978. And he had been back to jail a lot since then, including a thirty-day sentence in the D.C. jail. But he decided he should pay the fine this time.

(I had been arrested with Leszek in Wheaton, Maryland, at a rescue after an all-night vigil at the Sigma abortion mill. The vigils had been inspired partly by Vince Petersen, who emphasized that we really had to spend time praying before we acted. There was a rescue planned for January 22, 1981, the anniversary of the Supreme Court decision. We spent the night by the side of the road near the abortion mill, praying. That night, it sleeted. We sat on a little sheet under a little blanket while the ice came down. We sat there all night in the snow. In the morning, Leszek's beard was all ice. It seemed very logical then, but now I look back and wonder. Early in the morning, someone got stuck in the parking lot, spinning on the ice. Leszek went into the lot and helped, trespassing to help the driver. Later, we went in and blocked the door of the mill and got arrested for that.)

In the holding tank, Gay Laurienzo was really torn over her decision. She really wanted to refuse to pay a fine, but her father was putting a lot of pressure on her to pay, because he had been so worried about her going to jail. She submitted, but she kept saying how wonderful it would be to go to jail together and read the Bible together. When her fine was paid and she was released, she gave me her book on Saint Teresa of Avila.

Ginny Robertson and I refused to pay, so the two of us ended up going to jail together. We both felt that it was wrong to pay a fine if you could possibly refuse, unless you were under extreme pressure to pay because of family or some other solid reason.

So we were driven to the Baltimore city jail, a grimy Gothic castle. We went through all the slow, routine processing, surrendering our property and waiting while it was all recorded, item by item. Then we showered and got our jail clothes.

We were separated for several hours. Ginny was just eighteen, and they considered putting her in a separate cell or in a different part of the jail.

While they were deciding, they put me in a big cell all by myself, at the end of a hall. On one side of the hall, there were solitary confinement cells. Some of them were for trustees, some of them were for those who were insane and some of them were punishment cells. On the other side of the hall there were huge dormitory cells. In the middle, there was one guard station.

At the very end of one hallway there was a big empty tank, and that was where they put me. I was tired, so I lay down and went to sleep. When I woke up, there was another inmate with me. She was huge; she must have weighed three hundred pounds. I do not remember exactly how our conversation went, but I remember clearly that all of a sudden I knew I should be afraid of her.

Since then, I have met many homosexual women in prisons and jails. I have seen a few in jails, but there they are outnumbered by the others and are usually very low-key about themselves. But in prison they are in the majority—they are about 98 percent of the population. So they are very vocal, and they do not hide their activity. But this was my first exposure to jail, and this huge woman let me know what her interests were. I was scared stiff.

The noise in there was incredible. You can imagine what it must be like, with all those dormitory cells side by side. The woman right across from us was crazy, screaming and yelling all the time. I got to know her later. She had been a medical student, but she was in a car accident, and she lost one eye and went crazy. She was being held in this little holding cell, where she would scream and yell all day. It was noisy as could be. I figured that if I screamed, no one would hear me.

What saved me, after a quick prayer, was getting my cellmate to talk about herself. We were in there together for an hour or more until a guard finally wandered down that end of the hall. I jumped up and I said, "Oh, I need to talk to this officer."

I told the guard, "Really quickly, I need to get out of here."

She looked at us and said, "Oh, my God, I didn't know. You weren't supposed to be in here." She acted scared, and that was very reassuring, because it meant that she knew what the problem was. They got me out immediately, and then they put me with Ginny.

We were together in a huge dormitory cell, with eighteen or twenty other inmates. I got in a little trouble there almost immediately. There was a woman sitting on the cot next to mine. She had a magazine propped up, and I looked at it. Maybe I touched the corner, but I don't think so. Basically, I looked at it. She jumped on me, acted like she wanted to kill me. I said, "Oh, I'm sorry." She was really upset. I looked at her magazine: the crime of the century was committed there.

But most of the time it was not like that. Ginny and I would pray together most of the time, and the other inmates respected that. Some would come up to us in the middle of the night and ask us to pray with them. They did not want the other inmates to know that they were praying.

I remember one woman, called Legs, in particular. She was a prostitute, a tall, beautiful black girl who had had several abortions. She wanted us to pray that her husband would write her a letter. She talked a lot about her husband.

There was another girl whose brother had been murdered in the men's section of the jail, which was a couple of floors above us, earlier that year. The story was that he was killed by a guard. He was beaten up, thrown down the stairs, then brought back to his cell and hanged. She thought he had died before he got back to his cell. Soon after that, the guard was murdered on the street after work by friends of her brother.

She was really nice to us and prayed with us. And she was very upset with our being in jail. She kept saying, "Please don't come back." She said it was a horrible place, that we should not be there.

There was a great deal of violence and hostility between the guards and the inmates in the men's jail. There was not so much in the women's jail. One female guard had been stabbed by an inmate, and so the guards were very cautious.

In conversations, sometimes Ginny would put her arms around guards. I told her not to do that, because it's best for them not to allow it. If they relax, they can easily be betrayed and get hurt.

Ginny was a fresh-faced teenager, full of curiosity. She would ask people what they were there for. Some of them were there for some pretty awful things. I used to tell her, "Wait, and if someone tells you, great. If someone would like to talk and get it off her chest, great. But don't ask. Some lady might growl at you and jump down your throat, or you might hurt someone's feelings. Some will be smart enough to say, 'Listen, I don't want to talk about it.' But others might feel in a bind if you ask them. It's best not to." But she was so innocent and young and sweet, she always got away with it.

There were all kinds of inmates. We were fasting, just on water for the first week and a partial fast during the second week. Some of the other inmates wanted us to keep it up so that they could get our food. "Good fast, keep going! Can I have this; can I have that?" Others were really concerned about us, and they would tell us to eat.

Once, when we were standing in line for some reason, waiting for some paperwork that had to be done, there was a woman sitting on the floor next to me. I must have brushed against her, but I did not even notice it. I had not done anything at all, and all of a sudden, she was ready for a fight. She wanted to swing some fists. I apologized to her, and nothing happened. But there was so much hostility and anger there.

There was a time when everything just went crazy. It was as if everybody was suddenly claustrophobic. They started screaming and pounding on the walls; the whole cell went into chaos, just from tension, constant tension.

Of course, we all had lice, or "crabs". Everyone had to be washed down with different tar solutions. It was a really dirty jail.

Once, I woke up in the middle of the night to the cries from a woman in a different cell, right down the hall from my cell, who was evidently being brutally attacked. It sounded as if she was being sexually assaulted by several inmates. No one else woke up and said anything; it was just all quiet except for this woman. And so I jumped up and started banging against the bars and calling for the guard at the guard station. I called and banged and called and called, and I could hear the screams being muffled. She was being threatened, told that she had better not say anything.

I cannot imagine that the guards did not hear it. It was late, around 2:00 in the morning, and the only sounds were the screams. Eventually, a guard meandered down slowly. I said, "There's a woman being attacked in the other cell." She looked at me and meandered past, walked down and came back and said, "I can't see anything."

The victim had been threatened. The guard had not even asked if someone wanted to be put in different custody; she simply walked away, leaving the woman totally at the mercy of the people who were attacking her.

Our cell did not have any windows. But once a day, for maybe half an hour or an hour, we were allowed to walk the corridor between the cells. Inmates took turns walking, one cell at a time. One cell would be let out, and then when they were locked back in, the next cell would get out.

At the end of the corridor there was a window with slats, and we could look out those little tiny windows. We could see a little bit—the light posts in the road, and the highway with the bridge over it. I remember thinking, oh, gee, how nice to get in a car and drive out.

There was a Catholic priest there who came in to see us. He was the one who told me how bad things were at the men's prison. He was not able to go over there anymore, because the guards were hostile to him. They hated anyone who wanted to do anything for the inmates, because they hated the inmates. There was so much hostility and violence between the two groups!

He gave us contraband Communion a couple of times, slipped through the iron grid when a guard looked the other way. That was the first time I ever received my Lord by contraband. It had to be secret, because in the visiting room you weren't supposed to pass anything.

A priest could come for a service if it was set up through the chaplain ministry, but the whole thing had to be set up through the jail bureaucracy. He was not the prison chaplain.

There was a woman, a nun, in charge of prison ministry. She did a lot of service as a social worker, and she had a Communion service once a week. The service took about ten or fifteen minutes, with a couple of prayers and then Holy Communion. Once, she did not call me for Communion because I had a visitor. I was very upset when I found out about that.

I asked the priest who visited us if we could have Mass sometime, and he said he would love to do it, but that I had to get permission from the nun. I asked her and she said, "Oh, we don't want anybody inter-fering with our little community." The Holy Sacri-fice of the Mass: Can't a woman have it at least once a week? No, we don't want the community disturbed.

Generally, she was loved, because she gave out a lot of cigarettes and she did help the inmates socially. She was a very good social worker. A poor nun, but a very good social worker. It would have been nice if she could have combined the two. But she was definitely misled or had a misunderstanding of her role as a nun. She did not seem to know that the spiritual needs of people are far greater than any material needs.

We were in jail for two weeks, but it seemed like forever at the time. I must have become claustrophobic during that period, because it was just so compressed with people, so overcrowded, with no window. But we got released.

We had expected to be in for thirty days. We had each been fined three hundred dollars, and in Maryland, when you refuse to pay fines, you work them off at ten dollars per day. But then our attorney, Dan Bartolini, found that there was a fifteen-day ceiling and got us out.

One of the rescuers convicted with us was Marilyn Szewczyk. She ran several pregnancy aid centers in Maryland, which was the reason she felt she should not spend time in jail. She had been working to get us into a work-release program to work at the Crisis Pregnancy Center down at the shore, at Ocean City, Maryland. But we were released before that came through.

Getting out earlier than we had expected was a great feeling. Marilyn picked us up, and as we drove away, I remember seeing a gorgeous sunset.

7 Breaking the Injunction

It was hard to maintain momentum for rescues. People went their own ways, lived their own lives.

Before we even got started in St. Louis, at the beginning of 1980, Susan had gotten married and moved back to Delaware. Miriam and I stayed in St. Louis, living together at Jean Klocker's place. Jeannie was a court reporter, and she was out of town traveling most of the time. Jane Gibson also came and stayed with us.

That was the situation in the fall of 1980, when we were doing rescues with just a few people. There were just John Ryan, Laura Armstrong, Mike Reid, Miriam and I doing rescues. Ann could only do it rarely. Once in a while, when Jean came back to town and was free on a weekday, she would do a rescue with us. But that was about it. Sam would join us once in a while, but he was working during the week, too.

In 1981, Miriam and I went back and forth between St. Louis and Delaware. We started working with the people in Philadelphia, and we also did a few rescues in Maryland. Then Miriam met John Lademan and transferred to school in the Philadelphia area to be closer to him.

In 1982, I went back and forth by myself. When I was in St. Louis, I would stay with Jeannie. But that

year Jeannie was murdered, in a freak event that had
nothing to do with rescues.

When I was in St. Louis, I tried to do daily rescues
at one mill or another. On Fridays, I would join John
in Bridgeton, but other days I would go alone to Reproductive Health Services or Bridgeton. We got away
with it at RHS; for some reason they did not pull the
injunction on us. I guess they just did not want to
publicize the fact that people were ignoring the injunction. I think they were scared of that.

I left in the fall of 1982 and got involved with doing
rescues in Delaware and Pennsylvania. I told my
friends in St. Louis that I would be on the East Coast
but that if they decided they were going to break the
injunctions at Manchester or University City, I would
join them. I thought that breaking the injunction
would be the only way to ignite the movement. It was
rare that an abortion mill was able to get an injunction, and I thought we should show that we had only
contempt for such abuses of law, such blatant tyranny
as those injunctions.

In the summer of 1982, John Ryan called to let me
know that they were planning to break the injunction
that fall, in September, and to keep his promise to let
me know about it. I said I would be there. When I
arrived, there were just four people ready to act:
Samuel Lee, John Ryan, Ann O'Brien and myself.

John had begun to get a support group. A small
group of prolifers in the Bridgeton area had decided
to go out and pray the Rosary with him, to be the
John Ryan support group, just to make sure the
police did not beat him up too badly. Later, after he
got out of jail after breaking the injunction, they

became the core of John's Pro-Life Direct Action League.

In September, the four of us went to the Ladies Center in University City, and for a while we went there every week. It is a low building in a shopping mall and has since closed. They tried to reopen elsewhere in University City, but we kept them from doing that.

There were a lot of Rosaries on top of that roof. We went there at night to pray. We had a series of vigils there.

When we first broke the injunction, nothing happened, and we decided to keep doing it. I did one Wednesday rescue by myself, but then Samuel persuaded me that we should more or less stick together.

We went back the next Saturday, and then the next and the next. I missed one week, because I had something come up in the East. But we kept at it until November, when we were finally called into court and served with papers on our violation of the injunction.

Once again, the judge was a Catholic.

We waited around for our sentence, but he did not do anything, so I left town. The day after I left, he sentenced us. He did not bring us into court to sentence us—he just sentenced us and then called the newspaper and let them know. The first that Samuel heard about it was when a reporter called him to ask for a reaction to the sentence. Samuel said, "What sentence?" The reporter told him that he and Ann had each gotten 314 days in jail, and John Ryan and I had each gotten 225 days.

We got 15 days for the first rescue, 30 for the second, 45 for the third, 60 for the fourth, 75 for the fifth—and

Samuel and Ann got 89 for a sixth rescue. For each additional violation of the injunction, the judge was going to give 89 days.

We were all taken into custody. I had to go back right away to be taken in. But then we got out on an appeal.

In 1983, we lost the appeal. Luckily, I got to attend Miriam's wedding in May. In the beginning of June, we had to turn ourselves in.

Ann, John and Samuel turned themselves in together, and they were put on work release. But I was an hour late. As soon as I showed up in town, I went to see my lawyer, spoke with him for an hour and then went to the courthouse.

For some reason, the man in charge of the work-release program there asked me to promise not to go to an abortion mill while I was on work release. The other three had not been asked that. Of course I said I would not promise any such thing; I would not abide by it if it were stipulated. I was going to go to the abortion mill if I got a chance. So they told me that they would not give me work release.

I still do not understand how one little hour made such a difference. It had already been worked out I was going on work release, and I would work at Our Lady's Inn. But that was how it was.

They held me there in the county jail for two months, and then I was sent to the large facility at Gumbo. They kept thinking that I would eventually agree to the condition, but I never did.

During my time in prison, the judge kept saying that if we would agree to abide by the injunction, he would not bring us to trial for some other cases. The penalties for other violations were, of course, getting pretty stiff. But none of us would agree to that.

They thought they had us over a barrel. We were already doing time, and the judge said that while we were in jail, he was going to bring up these other cases. We would be convicted, the time would be added onto what we were already doing and we would forget what sunshine looked like. But none of us would agree.

The prosecutors were upset. Our attorney was upset, too. He wanted us to agree. None of us would. Eventually we just did our time, got released, then went back and broke the injunction again at the Ladies Center.

We were not backing down, and they realized that the long sentences were not going to do any good.

The sad thing was that we got little support. We thought that breaking the injunction would bring a lot of support, but the whole thing was too scary for some people. People were very cautious. Instead of showing strong support, showing that they were upset with the judge, they were careful not to picket the judge or the courthouse or the jail. Don't do this, don't do that, don't do anything. Don't even whisper. It was almost like Florida.

It seems to me that if someone is going to hit you hard, you should show that you are strong. I think we were being strong in prison, the four of us in jail. But we needed our supporters to show that.

Our supporters thought it would hurt us if they did anything. We tried to persuade them that they should go ahead and protest. But it was awkward. You cannot beg people to picket on your behalf. But we tried to let people know that they should not be cautious on our behalf; they should do whatever they wanted to do in support of us.

But the prevailing attitude was to keep cool and not do anything. In July, Dottie Shoenhorst came out. George Farrelly and Bob Moran came down from Philadelphia, and they had a vigil in front of the jail, with Jack and Jennie Kirsting and Dottie Shoenhorst. Half of the force was from out of state. That shows how bad it had gotten in St. Louis.

8 Gumbo

After we were arrested for violating the injunction and sentenced to months in jail, we all started serving our time at the St. Louis county jail in Clayton. But since I was not on work release, I was eventually shifted to Gumbo.

This was during the great heat wave of 1983. Over a hundred people died in the city, and there were emergency efforts to bring fans to people and things like that. The temperature was over one hundred degrees, and it got much hotter inside the prison—it was like a pressure cooker. The prison launched "Operation Sahara", in which they brought ice around every once in a while. Everybody spent as much time as possible in the shower.

The prison was a flat-roofed building with no air conditioning, and the women's cells were on the top floor. The heat just came right through the roof. Many people were afflicted with heatstroke and sent to the hospital.

It was really crowded in the dormitory cells. There were supposed to be only twenty inmates per cell, but there were close to forty. So people were sleeping on the floor in between the cots. Of course, that just increased the noise. When fights would break out, the guards would separate people by switching them from cell to cell or from dormitory to dormitory.

A few murderers were in there that summer. I remember one woman in my dormitory, really a horrible case. She was criminally insane. She had killed a seventeen-year-old boy she had gotten to know at a gas station where she had often bought gas. The murder was all filmed in a security-system videotape, and you could see him smiling and talking to her. All of a sudden she pulled out her gun and started shooting him. She shot him over a dozen times.

She was in jail when the Korean jet was shot down by the Soviets. She jumped up and down in front of the television, yelling and screaming, "There's going to be a nuclear war!" She was so thrilled. She thought it was fantastic and that the whole world was going to be blown up. She was all enthused about having a nuclear holocaust.

She was totally violent, totally volatile all the time. You couldn't leave her alone. I was there all through the fall, and she was there the whole time. I later read that she had been convicted and given a life sentence. It was good that they did not give her the death penalty.

One common form of violence was bouncing people. Somebody would pick up another person and bounce her on the concrete floor, kick her, drag her into the shower and bounce her in there. Really weird.

I never got bounced. I have found that prolifers are liked in prison. Christians are liked. Anyone who is halfway compassionate, halfway decent, halfway kind—even halfway—gets treated pretty well. The people who end up in prison for violent crimes or just for living a criminal life, or because they have been doing what they want to do, are not used to compassion, and they respond to it.

In the heat, with everyone lying around all day sweating and tempers hot late at night, you feel as if you are making some real sacrifices. You do not want to say that out loud, because you do not want to get too impressed with yourself. But inside you think, yeah, this is pretty rough.

One of the books I read that summer was Father Walter Ciszek's *He Leadeth Me*. It really brought home to me how little my sacrifice was and how little the sacrifice asked of us in the whole prolife movement and rescue movement has been. When I compare what we have been doing to save the babies to what the babies are suffering, it becomes clear that we have not done very much.

Father Ciszek's experience touched me. He was a Jesuit priest in prison for twenty years in Russia. The first five years, he was in solitary confinement, and his captors would torture him and harass him with questions. They would interrogate him all night and day. Sometimes he would be left alone for a couple of days, and they would not bother him at all. Then they would go after him for fifteen minutes on one day, and then nothing the next.

Father Ciszek's captors wanted to break him down psychologically. It went on and on, and eventually he was beaten. He signed some papers that said he was a spy for Rome. He just broke, he said. In his frail humanity, he got scared and could not take it anymore. He broke.

I was really touched by that, because I know how gentle God is with someone who just breaks. God is so very, very gentle with someone like that, but the person feels just devastated.

And yet, later on, Father Ciszek and other prisoners were able to do great things. He went to a labor camp, where he helped others to unload huge ships, carrying the cargo off ships on their backs. They had meager rations, one or two meals a day of watery soup or something like that. But they would give up those meals in order to fast. (That was when there was still a fast from midnight on before you could receive Communion.) They would try to get together for Communion and have Mass in the morning. Of course, that was a crime, a capital offense. So he and other prisoners risked death to go to Mass.

Sometimes they could not make it to Mass. They would go all day without food, doing hard labor, and then try to get to Mass in the evening. And if they did not make it then, they still kept fasting and tried again the next day. It was incredible to what lengths they would go out of respect for the Blessed Sacrament.

Their sacrifices for love of the Lord, their respect for the Blessed Sacrament, the sacrifices they made in fear and hunger, in jail and exhausted from hard labor—these are incredible. It makes you realize what real suffering is and what real love means.

They were cheerful under those circumstances, surrounded by traitors who would betray them. Some priests betrayed their people, and yet people kept their respect for the priesthood, even when a priest was a traitor. Of course, some were ready to choke the traitor to death themselves. But the love of the faithful ones was beautiful.

Things like that really inspired me while I was in Gumbo. They made me realize just what little sacrifices we have been asked to go through in the prolife movement. The prolife movement has not even begun to suffer.

There is a nun from the Philippines who wrote to me while I was in prison. She had been under house arrest during the years of Marcos' dictatorship because of her work for her people. During the Filipino revolution, she was one of those small, quiet nuns in the streets of Manila, out there stopping the tanks and marines. And she is one of the great prolife leaders of the country. She certainly has known what it means to suffer.

Here in America, we sue people for emotional distress if they insult us! We used to say, "Sticks and stones may break my bones, but names will never hurt me." You would think that people who follow Jesus would learn not to fear sticks and stones either. But in fact, here in America we are always discovering new ways that we can be injured—we are a nation of hypochondriacs.

The people who have suffered for their Faith understand what it means to take risks to protect babies. There is another nun, a former missionary to New Zealand, who was arrested there and tortured for a whole day until she was semiconscious, and then she signed some incriminating paper. Now she lives in Brazil, and she supports the rescue movement.

In Gumbo, I read about "victim souls", people chosen by the Lord to pray for the world and to feel the pain that is always there when love renews something that is broken.

Someone sent me a little booklet about a Portuguese girl named Augustina, who, sixty or seventy years ago, had to defend her purity by jumping out of a second-story window in her home. She broke her back but was not crippled immediately. She picked up a stick and chased the two men who were attacking her. Eventually she became paralyzed. Friends wanted her to go to Fatima for a cure, but she thought that God wanted her to be a "victim soul". She offered herself to God as a willing sacrifice, making her suffering a part of her prayer. The whole purpose of her life was to suffer for the conversion of sinners, and soon people started flocking to her home.

There was a period when she went through terrible pain and mental torment, and she thought that she was being attacked by the devil. She told God that she could not take any more, but he told her she could, so she did. In the end, after years of pain and torment, she died a very peaceful death. She said that the Lord assured her that her prayer and sacrifice had touched thousands of lives, helped thousands of people break away from shallowness and luxury and sin and turn to him.

When you read stories like that, you wonder how much you could endure. I thought that I could never go through the kind of torment that she described. It is not something to seek out. But you still recognize the challenge, and it provides a contrast to our modern horror of any kind of sacrifice.

I did not want anything like that, but still I found it very moving that there are people who offer themselves as victim souls, people whom God calls to be victim souls.

It was very stark, very challenging. It shook me up and deeply touched me.

I have heard of the idea since then. In fact, one of
the prolife activists in Philadelphia thinks her daughter is a "victim soul". The daughter lived only four
years, suffering with cancer.

The mother, Jean Neary, had started working
against abortion in Pennsylvania when it was still
illegal there. She reported abortionists, but the authorities would never prosecute.

She worked hard to persuade women to keep their
babies alive, and she took many girls into her own
home. She set up and advertised a crisis pregnancy
center, offering information about abortion to pregnant women. Of course, she was offering the truth,
not a pack of lies and a referral, so the abortion industry attacked her. A local newspaper printed her name
and address, with a picture of her and her house. She
got death threats and bomb threats, and her ads were
kept out of the phone book for a while.

Once, when a girl was going in for an abortion, this
woman told the Lord that she would accept anything
just to save that baby. Not long after that, her daughter developed cancer. The little girl suffered terribly,
but she knew and loved Jesus and his Mother Mary.
She would try not to cry with all the pain and would
try to "offer it up to Jesus".

A victim soul is a beautiful thing, a gift that the
Lord allows for some people who are willing to accept
that suffering.

But whatever you make of the concept, things like
that put our suffering in context. The heat in Gumbo
was a very slight sacrifice.

9 John Ryan, Alone

John Ryan was one of the four people jailed for breaking the injunction in St. Louis. He and Samuel Lee and Ann O'Brien had gotten work release, and they were in Clayton.

John has been arrested over four hundred times. For a couple of years, he was really the leader of the rescue movement across the country. He got involved through his father, who was very active in prolife work. As a teenager, John used to attend meetings with his father. He told me that he always felt that with killing going on, people should be trying to stop it where it was occurring. So when rescue missions first came to St. Louis, he read about them in the newspaper and thought, yes, this is what needs to be done. In fact, this is what I should be doing. But he was not ready to jump right into it. He did not go to his first rescue mission until 1980. From 1978 on, there were rescues every once in a while, but he did not know any of the people who did them.

In 1980, Dottie Shoenhorst got involved in rescues. She was a neighbor of one of John's friends, and that was the kind of person-to-person contact that made recruiting work. He got involved through her, and in the spring of 1980 he was arrested for the first time.

John participated in almost every rescue from then on. He stood firm about not cooperating with the injunction, not going along with the lawyers when they wanted us to move from Manchester.

John never considered himself a leader. He just continued to do rescues and do rescues and would not stop doing them. Even when everybody else stopped for one reason or another, he continued to do them all by himself. He did not try to be a leader; he just felt that he had to do rescues, so he kept on doing them and wishing others would also.

John prayed that the leaders like Samuel Lee would come back and do rescues. But Samuel had gotten involved in pregnancy aid and legal work. Samuel Lee's history was very different from that of most rescuers, who go through legislation and lobbying and all that and then come around to believing rescue is the only way to stop the killing. Sam started with doing rescues and then went the other route. Now he works on legislation, works with lawyers, tries to pass bills and all that kind of thing. But John had discarded that approach, not convinced that it could do very much good.

Throughout 1981, John went out to Bridgeton over and over, usually all by himself. He would sit there and pray the Rosary and block the door. Eventually, other people began to go out there, too, to protect him, just to be a witness. When someone was watching, he was much safer from the police or sometimes the boyfriends, the fathers of the babies, who might beat him up.

The courts were not punishing John, so the police did it themselves. Sometimes he would be worked

over with billy clubs. I was with him at one rescue
when both his wrists were damaged, so that for a long,
long time he had no feeling in them. He and I were
the only ones there to block the door. Pam Bizaillion
was there to counsel. She was six or seven months
pregnant at the time. When she heard John screaming, she just hid around the corner, petrified.

We were already handcuffed, sitting on the ground,
when the police came and told us to walk out. John
explained to the officer that he could not walk out,
that if he walked out he would be cooperating in his
removal and babies would die. There were two officers
there, but the one who did all the talking was a big
guy who was new there. He said, "Listen, you made
your point, but now you're going to walk out."

John said, "I'm sorry, I can't."

The officer said, "Oh, yes, you can. You have control
of your legs."

John answered, "Precisely so; that's why I cannot
walk out."

The large officer said, "Oh, you will walk out." The
week before, this same officer had threatened to bring
John by way of the hospital if he did not walk out,
and then after a great deal of torture they went ahead
and dragged him. So again he reminded John that he
might have to go to the hospital on his way to the
police station. Then he started to choke John with his
billy club against John's throat. At the same time, the
other officer was twisting the handcuffs into John's
wrist and twisting John's thumb back. John just
started screaming. You could hear his screams all
through the whole building.

You have to get a clear picture of this. The abortion

mill is right in the middle of something like a medical park, with nice music playing in the hallway and potted plants growing everywhere. John had been thrown into the plants right by the abortionist's door so often that the plants were all bent over, dying or dead. And there were little decorative pebbles from around the plants all over the walkway right around the abortionist's office. You could tell that there had been a skirmish there.

Once when John was being taken out, he grabbed hold of the drapes in the abortionist's large windows facing out into the common area inside the building. The curtains came down, and the abortionist never put them back up again. So when prolifers were outside praying the Rosary and holding up signs that women in the waiting room could see, they could not close the drapes.

Anyway, this time John was on the ground screaming, and people inside the mill could see him and hear him. Right across the hall, there was a dentist's office, and there were other medical offices all down this little walkway; the whole building was full of medical offices. They could all hear him, especially those nervous patients at the dentists waiting to see whether their teeth were going to be drilled.

After a little bit, the officers stopped and said again, "Now you're going to walk", and John said again, "I can't."

The officers did it all again, and of course he screamed some more.

I just sat there. I was really shocked. We had been roughed up before and the arresting officers had been intentionally brutal. But not like this.

Shortly thereafter, John Ryan had his hands cuffed behind his back, was picked up by two policemen and dropped on his face before being tossed in the wagon.

I did not know what I could do. I thought that if I pleaded for John, they would hurt him more, because they would think that they were getting to us. I remember thinking, "Just beg them", and then thinking, "But that would be worse. They'll do it longer if they think that I might break down and cry. Maybe they will think they can convince John to walk if they see that it's upsetting me."

So I did not do anything; I just sat there. Pam hid around the corner. The people in the other offices tried to pretend nothing was going on, but we would see them peeking.

While the police were torturing John, he would scream. In between, when they stopped for a few seconds, he begged them to stop. But when he saw that they were not going to stop, he gave up pleading, and then between screams he said, "God bless you." He kept saying, "God bless you", as they were torturing him. He screamed, then said, "God bless you", then screamed again and said, "God bless you."

Finally one cop said, "Let's just take him; let's just take him." So they hauled him out through the double glass doors, using him as a battering ram to open the two doors, and threw him in the police car. Then they got me and threw me in.

In the police car, John apologized to me and the cops for screaming. That broke my heart more than the screaming.

I did not do anything then, but I know what to do in the future. The normal thing to do is to get up and run, and then they have to chase after you. Or I could have kicked through the window of the mill, since no one was by the windows inside. I didn't think of doing that then; my brain was just blank. But I noticed that no women were by the window. If I had kicked it in and then gone into the abortion mill, they would have had to go after me.

For the next few weeks, when John went to the mill, his whole body would shake. If you just touched his wrists, it was excruciatingly painful to him. The next week, the police did not try to torture him. But they picked him up by his cuffs, and he was in agony.

That was one case we wanted to see go to court. It concerned pure out-and-out torture, not just the pain tactics that the police often use; it was really very bad. We wanted to bring it to court, but whenever we tried to file a complaint, the police refused to take our report. They said we had to come back some time when we were not under arrest. When we got released, we said that we were not in an arrest mode. But they still said, no, come back on a different day.

But whenever we were in the area, of course, we went to the abortion mill. Eventually, John did go on a different day, but they never did anything. They lost the papers and this, that and the other thing. Finally, we just gave up.

Generally, complaints against the police are not important. In fact, they can be a distraction when babies are being torn to pieces, and prolifers are whimpering about cuts on their fingers. Generally, we should not put our time and energy into that; we should just take whatever the police do and never complain or file a complaint. We should try to show by our actions that we are respectful of legal authority, that we are not just angry troublemakers, that we are trying to save lives. That should be the message of our silence and endurance.

But if the police endanger someone's life or if they are clearly going out of rational control, then we should not ignore that. If an officer beats up a white man with powerful friends, what will he do to a poor black man? We cannot ignore all their attacks.

For a year John's hand was numb, and he could not tell when his fingers closed on something except by looking at them. If he bumped his hand, even when he was just buttoning the cuff on his shirt sleeve, the pain was terrible.

He was afraid of being handcuffed and dragged. He was so scared he was almost sick to his stomach. But he kept coming to rescues. And after I moved East, he was by himself for a little while, before a support group built up. He had been hit with billy clubs and roughed up for a long time, but after that incident, people started coming out to support him.

Someone else who used to do rescues there was Mike Reid. He was incredibly strong. He could stand in a doorway with cops pulling on him from the front and pushing him from the back, and he would just stay there. He worked out, lifted weights. He was not like that green cartoon character, the Hulk. He was not that big. But he was really strong. When we were clinging onto him, and when he was holding onto us, we had it good. You could never get him out of the door.

Mike was an incredible person—he was a great man. He really did love the babies.

Once Mike did something he should not have done, something we should never do. He did it out of compassion, but it was still a mistake. The cops had red faces,

and they were hitting him on his arms with a billy
club—bam, bam, bam—and he was just standing
there. Other officers were yanking on him. Then he
started feeling sorry for an officer, and I think he
relaxed a little and let them pull him out from the
door. Mike has a sensitive conscience. He felt torn and
talked about it to a friend later.

It is one thing to decide ahead of time that you will
resist the killing only by an appeal to the heart of
each participant, beginning with the child's mother
and ending with the police. I do not have any problem
with people going limp, if that is their decision. But
to decide that you will make every effort short of phys-
ical attack on another person to stay there between
the killer and his victims, and then to give up out of
false kindness to the police—that is just wrong. And
I know that Mike would say the same thing now; he
did it only once, before he thought about it.

As far as I know, Mike Reid was the first person to
disarm the murder weapons. He did it by himself. The
prolifers, including the rescuers, really jumped down
his throat. He just took the weapons apart, out in
Bridgeton. But it never came to trial, because the
abortionists did not want the publicity, did not want
people thinking about what one man had done to the
weapons.

John Ryan was not a leader in the first few years
after he started rescuing. He was persistent, and he
became an inspiration. But he did not want to be a
leader. But in the beginning of 1984 when he got out
of jail after serving over seven months for breaking
the injunction, he decided he had to do some organizing. Samuel had gone back to the legal and political

John Ryan and others at a rescue at Rocky Mountain Planned Parenthood in Denver, 1986.

branch of the prolife movement, and there was no one else there ready to take charge.

John turned to the support group that had come out to Bridgeton with him to make sure he did not get hurt, and asked for their help in putting together a new organization, the Pro-Life Direct Action League. He started giving talks and recruiting.

The police had a lot of respect for John. Once, when I was arrested and refused to walk, a cop told me that I should walk, because "John Ryan walks out, and no one is a better prolifer than John Ryan." But it was the same cop who had beaten him up, lying to get me to cooperate. He didn't recognize me, since I rarely was in St. Louis now. Still he was right about that: no one is a better prolifer than John Ryan.

John built the Pro-Life Direct Action League from nothing to a viable group. Eventually they were doing rescues at least three times a month. The people there are very loyal to John, because he is very selfless, very humble. And he had a great sense of humor, always breaking the constant tension. He was a dedicated, staunch, faithful Catholic, right down the line on everything, including the tough one, birth control. He had a great love for the Church.

John was always very understanding. Although he was scathingly critical of the police decision to remove us, he was very good with the individual officers. He would point things out to them, explaining that they should not remove us. But he got along well with them. Many of them respected him.

John knew we needed to have an organization to push rescues after Samuel Lee dropped out and the rescue movement subsided. But for a long time he just kept doing the rescues by himself. Finally, he decided it had to be done and he had to come forward, since no one else was willing to do it.

He turned out to be a very good leader. He put out a good newsletter, with good articles and humor in them. He would never judge others and would not push people past their limits, never make them feel they should do more than they could. He was humble about his own accomplishments and sacrifices.

10 Martin Luther King's Seminary

I first met the Philadelphia activists in 1978, when I was living in Delaware with Susan and a friend named Francis (Frannie) Mulvena. Every once in a while we would picket the abortion mills and abortion hospitals in Delaware. And every once in a while Frannie would take me over to Chester, Pennsylvania, and we would picket near the Crozer-Chester Memorial Hospital, where they killed babies. There I met Bob Moran, who had been faithfully praying and picketing there for years. Bob and his wife had fifteen children.

The abortion mill was in a building that had been part of an old Baptist seminary. When the seminary closed, the hospital bought the land and buildings and used them for housing medical students and other purposes. One building looked like an old chapel but had actually been the library. That had become the abortion mill.

Martin Luther King studied there before he went to Boston University. In the rooms where that great teacher of nonviolence had read Scripture and prepared to be a minister, doctors had started killing babies. In time it became a focal point of the struggle to use peaceful and nonviolent tactics to protect babies from discrimination and death.

In the summer of 1981, we had a couple of rescues

in Delaware. In 1982, when I came East, I wanted to plan some more rescues in Delaware. But the regular sidewalk counselors and picketers said that I could not do any more rescues there. They said that if Miriam and I did, they would not come out anymore.

That put a lot of pressure on us, and I was really depressed about it. But we were not that far from Chester. We thought that we would ask Bob Moran if he would mind if we had a rescue at the mill where he counseled and picketed and prayed.

We looked up his number and prayed that he would agree. In fact, we went to a prayer meeting that night. Then we called Bob, and I asked him, really tentatively: "Bob, my sister and I wanted to do a rescue in Delaware, but the local people don't want us to. Some put a lot of pressure on us, saying that they would quit, you know, and not come out to the abortion mill if we do it. But is there any way—would you ever mind if perhaps while you all are picketing, or even sometime when none of you are there, my sister and I would go up and block the doors?"

"Wonderful! Great!" he said. "It's like Christmas!" He got all excited; he couldn't believe it. "Oh, please, this is wonderful. Please, please do." I asked if it would be okay if we came that Saturday. He said, "Yes, yes, we're going to call some people. This is wonderful; this is just great."

Later, we found out that the numbers there had been dwindling. There were just a few people picketing every week. But that Saturday when we showed up for the rescue, the sidewalk was packed with people. Bob got everybody to come out.

So Miriam and I blocked the doors. We were running

around because there were two of us to block three doors—run to this door, run to that door, run to the basement door. The people on the sidewalk were singing and praying and calling out information to us, when someone pulled into the parking lot. They were not planning to join the rescue; they were just supporting us.

Eventually Miriam and I got arrested.

We got to counsel quite a few women. We kept them out, pretty much, until the security guard came down. He would try to push us away, and then someone from the inside would try to open the door, but as soon as they opened the door, we would try to get in. They would close the door immediately, which was fantastic. We did not get in, but nobody else did, either. When they closed the door on us, they closed the door on the mother, too. Finally, they pushed us out of the way to let a mother in the basement, before the police came.

This went on for three Saturdays in a row. The picketers kept coming back, and the group kept growing.

When we got released, the support people would take us out to eat.

The Pennsylvania people are great. The Delaware people were consistent for year after year after year of sidewalk counseling. They are tremendous and good people. But they really did not understand rescues, did not want anything to do with rescues. The Pennsylvania people did. They just loved it.

People sometimes ask if rescues ever get violent. I can remember only one or two times when I saw someone almost get violent. The second time we were at the Chester killing place was one of them.

We were going for the doors, and an abortion staffer was yanking us back. We went back and forth. Then a guard got into it, and he tried to keep Miriam down. It looked as if he was kicking her. I don't think he was, but he kept working his knee into her to hold her. She was on the ground, right in front of the door. People in the street thought that he was kicking her, because they could see his legs moving. George Farrelly was calling out to him to stop. The Pennsylvania people don't like to see women get beaten up.

John Beck started coming across the lawn to help, and for a minute it looked really bad for that guard. It looked as if John Beck might really grab him. But he stopped. We kept saying no, and finally he stopped himself. And then the other prolifers pulled him back.

Ever since, that guard has been really careful.

There was a similar incident in St. Louis. There is a rescue couple there, Jim and Barb Howard. They were in their early forties at the time. They had eight children, including twins, all nice children. They were very much in love, and he always called his wife "my bride". They could have been newlyweds on their honeymoon.

Once Jim saw Barb being roughed up by the police. He started to charge after them, but everybody grabbed him. A whole group of rescuers had to grab him, because he just went charging. He was not going to let anybody get rough with his wife. I had seen him get beaten up before. I saw him flipped once, knocked down and flipped all the way over. That was okay with him; he just lay there. But he could not stand to see anyone touch Barb!

Jane Gibson's spiritual director, Father Ong, tried to caution her about the rescue movement, saying that just radical kids were involved. We all scratched our heads over that. Janie told him that the majority of the rescuers were established middle-aged people with businesses. The movement started with university students, like the seminarians. But when they announced the campaign in 1980, the people who gravitated to it were mainly middle-aged, married people, with young kids. In Maryland young married couples predominated, but in St. Louis more were middle-aged. In Philadelphia, they ran the gamut.

When we started in Chester, Pennsylvania, in 1982, Miriam and I did rescues at Crozer-Chester three times. The third time we got arrested twice. After we were released, we went right back to the abortion mill, and then they held us.

After a second arrest on the same day, the judge was not going to let us go until we agreed not to go back. He said that if we agreed not to go back, they would let us out of jail, but he was going to hold us until we agreed.

Every day the judge would call the jail and ask if we had changed our mind and agreed not to go back, and we said no. Every day, he said he was concerned about us. He was getting a lot of pressure from people. He was in a little borough. So he said that he was very concerned, that he cared about us, and so on. He told us that he asked the warden about us every day.

Sometimes he would just ask the warden to convey his messages of concern, but sometimes he would call us up, and the guards would let the call through.

But he always asked if we would agree not to go
near the abortion mill, and he continued explaining
that he had no choice but to keep us there until we
agreed.

We kept saying no, and after several days the injunction came down. The injunction ordered people to stay
off the property, and it limited picketers to no more
than ten people a couple of feet apart.

After eight days, it was beginning to be clear that
we were not going to promise to stay away from the
place where our little brothers and sisters were being
killed. Keeping us in jail was not going to extract a
promise, so he should let us go.

Bob wanted to see the judge to point out to him that
with the injunction he did not need to extract our
promise. The situation had changed somewhat. If we
went back on the property or did anything there that
would violate the injunction, then we would go back
in jail for that.

But he could not find the judge. He went down to
the courthouse and all over town but could not find
him. He was not getting any cooperation. It seemed
that nobody knew where the judge was.

Bob is a smart man. What he decided to do was to
break the injunction himself. He drove right up to the
mill, where he was very well known. Everybody there
knew him, because he led the picketing there year
after year. He just stopped his car and walked right
into the hospital. That got their attention.

Police and guards came from everywhere. Bob did
not get more than a few feet inside before they surrounded him. "What do you want?" they asked.

He said, "I want to see the judge."

They put him in a car right away and whisked him off to the judge. When he saw the judge, he explained what he had been doing at the door of the hospital— just looking for someone who could tell him where the judge was—and then settled down to business. He explained that with the injunction the situation was different, and they did not need to extract our promise. The judge seemed to concur, and they released us. Bob came up to the prison and picked us up, and we left that day.

The night after we got out, a team of lawyers told us that they had met and decided to fight the injunction, and they had made some decisions about how to proceed.

Miriam and I went down to Crozer-Chester Hospital with Bob Moran and walked on the side of the road that was enjoined. But the lawyers told us not to do that and said that they would not stay on the case if we did. They truly felt they were doing what was best for winning the case for the babies by stopping rescues themselves. There is always much conflict among pro-lifers.

The lawyers said that they were going to fight the injunction, and they were going to win. And when they won, we would be able to have a table right inside the door of the mill where we could hand out literature. But they said that if we kept getting arrested, they would not be able to do it. It would jeopardize the case.

That always seemed crazy to me. If you abide by an injunction, they just say, "Hey, this injunction is doing what it's supposed to do, keeping these people under wraps, keeping them from doing what we don't

want them to do. There are just a few of them left out
there, and they are no trouble." It seems clear that
abiding by something is not going to help overturn it.
But reason aside, there was a lot of pressure at that
time not to break the injunction, because doing so
might hurt something.

The numbers of picketers had been shrinking, and
not much was going on in front of the hospital. Then
all of a sudden, we had all these people out picketing,
and lawyers out working, and there was going to be
a big injunction hearing. It was, for many, hope at
least.

In court, the rhetoric was beautiful, and it was a
real boost for the babies. But at the same time, there
were no rescues going on, because we were abiding
by this injunction, and that went on for two years.

Miriam and I had to go out of state to do rescues,
almost like Delaware again. The people loved the idea
of rescues, but they were not ready to do them themselves, and Miriam and I were not leaders.

Jack O'Brien had us come out to speak at the parish
church in Westchester, Saints Peter and Paul. We
talked, but Miriam was mild and timid, and I did not
know how to express myself very well, either. I was
not a leader.

We were hoping that someone would step forward
to organize some rescues. I felt that if we could just
explain it properly, somebody would say, "Hey, this
is great, let's do it", and organize it, the way it happened in St. Louis. But no one did, and that was the
end of it.

I would go to Maryland to do a rescue once in a
while, or go back to St. Louis and do it, or just do

the regular prolife work—lobbying and picketing and so on.

Eventually we got tried for the arrests at Crozer-Chester. There were twelve counts, four from each arrest. We had a jury trial that lasted for five days.

I did a terrible job on the stand. Miriam did well. That was not just my opinion; the lawyers agreed.

During the trial, the prosecution put the wrong policeman on the stand. He was not the arresting officer. There were some photographs of the officer reading something to us, and it looked as if he was telling us to leave. But a different officer was there on the witness stand.

When we took the stand, the prosecutor asked us what the arresting officer was saying in the photo. I said I did not remember. We were thinking about the babies, and there was a woman there that very day who was dragged up the steps, crying. She was listening to us, and we were talking to her and handing her literature, and she really did not want to go in there. She kept tripping, but her boyfriend kept yanking her back to her feet. She was crying, pleading with him, repeating, "I don't want to go in; please don't; I don't want to go in." But she got dragged in that door, and they "took care" of her. I remember her very well.

Later that morning, when we were sitting in the doorway, they had already gotten her in. It seemed that there were a lot of police that day, but we were still thinking about that poor woman. That was when the arresting officer talked to us, and the photographer got a picture of him telling us something. But when they asked me what he said, I did not remember what he said. I remembered this woman.

Then the prosecutor asked what I thought the officer was saying. I answered that I was sure they were telling us that we were violating something or other, that we shouldn't be here and so on.

The prolife attorneys gave summations explaining that we were saving lives, that saving lives is legal even on private property, that they could acquit us even if we had broken a few meaningless statutes in light of the circumstances. They were just beautiful.

The proabortion prosecutor presented his case, explaining that we did not have any right to be there.

The judge, named Clement McGovern, was a Roman Catholic and also an ordained deacon. He used to go to daily Mass, and we saw him every morning during the trial. Every morning we would go to morning Mass and he would be there, and we would all go to Communion together, and then we would be in court before him. So we were shocked when he gave his charge to the jury.

In Judge McGovern's final instructions to the jury, he said: "You have heard the defense counsel talk about God's law and man's law. Well, I'm telling you right now, that you cannot consider anything but the laws of this commonwealth. You cannot consider God's law." Or words to that effect.

Here he is, a daily communicant, divorcing his life from God's law, and telling free citizens of the United States to set aside their faith when they come into a courtroom. I could hardly believe it. I have heard since then that he still holds the same position. I was shocked.

At that point I did not care what happened next. It was so disgusting. How can a Catholic judge be so blind? In the encyclical *Casti Connubii,* Pope Pius XI said that the blood of innocent children killed by abortion "cries to heaven for vengeance". The Pope did not say that to poor women scared into a corner and considering desperate escapes. He addressed those words to legislators and judges, who are obliged to protect the innocent.

When the jury came out, we looked over and one young man smiled. So I was sure we were going to be acquitted, because a juror would not smile if they had decided to convict us. Everyone else had the usual stony face, but there was one smile.

Then the jury announced their verdict. There were twelve counts that they had to read off, and for each they responded: not guilty, not guilty, not guilty, not guilty.

We learned later how the jury came to their decision. Instead of saying, "We darn well will consider God's law!" they used a technical point. They were told to consider this ruling and that section of the law and all kinds of things. But in the end, it was simple for them. The cop on the stand was not the arresting officer. And that was it.

The judge was really amazed. You could see the shock on his face. He had not expected that we would be acquitted. Even though the jury found us not guilty, he preached at us, with more of the same nonsense about blind obedience to the letter of the law. It was probably the speech he had planned to give us before he sentenced us to jail, and he went ahead with it even though we were acquitted.

A week later, we were out at Crozer-Chester. It was cold and snowing a little. We were passing out literature to cars driving past. A man stopped and said that he had been one of the jurors. He had come out there because it had been bothering him. He was the one who told us what had happened in the jury room.

At first, eleven wanted to acquit us and one to convict us. But the majority convinced the one to acquit us. He said that he had been the holdout.

He said that the jury decided that they did not know what the arresting officer in the photograph was saying to us. He had argued that it was obvious what a policeman would be saying. But the rest of the jurors insisted that they had no right to presume—for all they knew, he could have been asking for a date. That, a technicality, was what got us off.

Not much more happened with rescues in Philadelphia for a couple of years. But Jack O'Brien kept reading material from the Prolife Nonviolent Action Project (PNAP) in Maryland, and he decided to have one of their speakers come up. At that time, PNAP was trying to recruit a thousand people for a rescue in Maryland. After that talk, and especially after the rescue itself, in May 1984, the Philadelphia activists started organizing rescues.

John and Mike Cornelly were very interested in starting rescues in New Jersey, near Philadelphia, but they only did a few. It never did catch on. To this day John is bogged down with family responsibilities. The southern New Jersey area just did not ignite. Of course, there were some people who got involved, like George and Tina Krail, but they are pretty much by themselves. Joe Scheidler gave a powerful talk there, and he got some people excited about activism. But it was not so much about rescues, just about getting on the streets, doing something more than talking.

St. Louis is a puzzle, too. I expected that when the rescue movement started blazing nationwide St. Louis would be ignited again, since there was so much action there years ago. But that has not happened. Perhaps if there is a really fervent movement that dies, that discourages people from starting up again. They say, well, we tried it once.

In Philadelphia, things really got started when Jack started organizing. He prayed about it, thought about it and realized it was important to do.

When Miriam and I were first in jail, he tried to talk us out of any further action that would lead to trouble. He wanted us to get out of jail and stay out.

His heart was touched, though, when he had people up from PNAP to talk in his parish. The meeting started with a song, followed by a good talk. After that meeting, many of the Philadelphia prolifers went to a rescue in Gaithersburg, and they saw what could be done to protect babies.

That rescue was organized by Harry Hand and PNAP. There were about two hundred people there, gathered at the Uptown Women's Clinic, Alan Ross' abortion mill. As the morning progressed, it seemed pretty clear that the abortionist had backed off and there would be no killing. But everybody stayed alert, making sure. People were lined up in rows, with arms linked, facing toward the door of the mill but not blocking it. They were ready to move if that became necessary.

Late in the morning, a woman approached the group and told the counselors who spoke with her that she was there for an abortion. So 140 people blocked the door in fifteen seconds. When they were all in place and the police were starting to move in to arrest people and the cameras were starting to roll, she got in front of the group and said she was there for a routine checkup, and she wanted to keep her baby. So everybody applauded and got out of her way.

Of course, she was a shill. She was in and out in ten minutes. After she came out, prolifers overheard her telling a police officer that she had called a friend and urged her to come to the mill; she urged her to tell the counselors that she was there for an abortion and to stick to her story, so that everybody would get arrested. Apparently, she had wanted to have the TV cameras show prolifers blocking the way of a woman who had legitimate business there, but her plan did not work. Her second plan also failed; her friend did not come to the mill.

During the minute before she changed her story, police arrested two people, Rod Smith and Dr. John O'Keefe. The leaders by the door did not see the arrests right away. When the officer who arrested Dr. O'Keefe saw that the situation was changing, he quietly took the handcuffs back off, and pretended that nothing had happened. Dr. O'Keefe was free.

Rod was taken away, though, and booked. The criminal charge was not serious, but Rod was a security guard, and his boss took a dim view of any arrests and fired him. But then Dick Hafer, a cartoonist and political satirist, intervened to help Rod, and he persuaded Rod's boss to take him back.

Rod said that he learned a lesson about courage that day. He had wavered in his decision about joining the rescue, and even at the mill he was still debating. So when everybody suddenly blocked the door, he hesitated and was one of the last people to join the blockade. That meant that he was on the edge of the group—and was the first arrested.

But Rod insisted that it was a blessing in his life. He was scared at first, but tried to put his trust in the Lord, and he learned a lot from it.

The effect on the Philadelphia people was very powerful. It was the first taste that most of these people had of rescue. There were many of them who had come down just to observe, tentative even about supporting it. But when the order came to link arms and get ready to block the door, it was electrifying. All of a sudden there was an emergency, and people were doing the obvious thing about it. It seemed that a child might be in danger, and adults were moving fast to protect the child. The people who had come to watch linked arms and blocked the door without hesitation.

I got arrested when I decided to check and make sure that there was no killing. I saw an opportunity to get inside the mill, and I went in. Roland Markun followed me, so I would not be alone in there, and we were arrested.

Tom Herlihy, a prolife activist from the Bronx, was there with his brothers. He felt very strongly that it was a mistake to get all those people together ready to risk arrest and then not have them arrested. It was interesting in later months that when people were talking about large rescues, they skipped Gaithersburg, because it was a success, with no deaths, no exploitation and almost no arrests.

From the very beginning there has been some disagreement about exactly what we should emphasize at the abortion mills. Tom's concern about no arrests was an example. Rescues do many different things, affect people in many different ways. The folks at PNAP were prepared to call it a success if no babies were killed or women abused that day. But Tom wanted to "confront the system", as well as accomplish those objectives. He saw clearly how difficult it was to get 140 people together for a rescue, and he wanted them all to see their power in a confrontation with the courts that had decided to kill babies.

Tom came down to work with PNAP that summer, and when there was a similar situation developing for a rescue in November, he made sure there was an alternate plan. On November 17, there was another large rescue at the same place, and again the abortionist canceled all the killing. So the group declared victory there, and immediately moved to another location. They had forty-seven people, including seventeen clergy, arrested for blocking the doors of an abortion clinic in Wheaton.

While Tom was there, the first "Baby Doe" went into jail in Montgomery County. The man was arrested at the Uptown abortion mill, and he spent a week in jail by himself. He was released without giving his name.

The rescue in Gaithersburg, even without the experience of arrest, really impressed Jack O'Brien. When he came back, he said he was very impressed that everything was so orderly, everybody was so obedient, following directions, and everything was so controlled. Until then, he thought it was something that

*Joan Andrews, Tom Herlihy, John Ryan and others
at a rescue in St. Louis, 1986.*

we should pray about and consider, but I think he was not convinced it was the way to go until he had experienced it.

In St. Louis also, some people were totally against rescues when they first heard about them. They dismissed them as "liberal propaganda". But when they saw one, they were convinced that it was the right thing to do. All they had to do was see it; that was where the conversion took place.

The next key event for the Philadelphia group was at the national Right to Life convention in Kansas City. Jack O'Brien did not go, but Mike McMonagle, one of the prolife leaders at the eastern end of the state, went. Mike was already enthusiastic about rescues. He had gone to the May 19 rescue. The Kansas City events made him even more firm in his decision to promote rescues.

Before the convention started, Joe Scheidler announced publicly that prolifers were going to close all the mills in Kansas City. But when we had a planning meeting, there was a lot of hesitation. At first, it seemed that it was a foregone conclusion that we were going to do rescues there. But then someone suggested that maybe we should all go home and do our rescues at home. After all, that was where we had our strongest support, our families. Perhaps we were most responsible for our own immediate neighbors, not for people in Kansas City.

At first, it was all decided except the details. Then suddenly the details included the question: Are we going to do this?

Finally someone asked John Ryan what he thought. He said, "What would I say to a woman who had her baby killed and knew I was in town, and she asked me why I did not do anything for her and her baby?" He made us all ask ourselves about the women facing abortion. How could we ask them to make sacrifices when we ourselves were willing to make only limited sacrifices?

He asked how could we say, "Oh, I'm sorry. Your children are in danger and you're in need of help, but we're going to do rescues when we get back home. It will be more convenient for us, and we won't have to come back for trial."

He said firmly that he was going to do a rescue.

There were some women from Women Exploited by Abortion (WEBA) standing there, listening and observing. They urged us to act, and their words meant a lot to everybody there. Nancyjo Mann spoke, and her words were really powerful. She said that if anyone had been there when her baby was in danger, the baby would be alive right now.

So the group decided to go ahead with a rescue. But the next day, it turned out that all that agony was for nothing; the mills closed. Over a hundred prolifers went prowling through Kansas City looking for anyone who might be planning to kill a baby, but the city was peaceful.

That success led to the "Kansas City pledge", an informal pledge that many rescuers took: whenever prolifers gather in large numbers, they will protect babies. It would not happen any more that prolifers would gather and talk and talk, while babies were dying in the same city on the same day. From that day forward, rescues would always be a part of prolife conventions.

The Kansas City convention was also a crucial factor in starting rescues in Philadelphia, because Mike's commitment was strengthened by it. Mike was president of the Southeast Pennsylvania Coalition for Human Life. Usually groups are big if their name is small, and small if their name is big, but the coalition was pretty influential anyway. Mike was a real leader. At that time, he was still working as a nuclear engineer; since then, he has put everything else aside to work for the babies.

Jack O'Brien just had a parish group, at Saints Peter and Paul in Westchester. But he is the one who started reading about rescues and organizing them. And he has a reputation as a man of prayer. Jack is a natural leader, and Mike is a natural organizer. They work together very well. Mike has since gone to work with Randy Terry at Operation Rescue, doing great work there.

The first eastern Pennsylvania rescue was the weekend of July 4, 1984, in Paoli. There were hundreds of picketers all over the place. They were not supposed to be off the sidewalk, but they went wherever they wanted to go—all over the parking lot and inside the building.

Those outside got a good opportunity to talk to the mothers and some fathers. The whole rescue group of about twenty people went inside, surprising police patrols and the abortion mill staff. People knelt down inside and outside the killing place and prayed.

There were two state representatives from nearby, Joseph Pitts and Peter Vroon, both solidly prolife. They talked to Jack, who was leading the rescue, and they went back and forth between him and the police for a long time.

Jack said that we would leave if we could get a solid commitment that the place would close down for the rest of the day. But they were not willing to do that, so the discussion went back and forth for hours. The police officers stood around outside the abortion mill. In the end, the police decided they had to arrest us, and they took nineteen people. The prolifers were not disturbed by that—except that it was wrong, and they knew that. But they were not afraid or upset.

Police had come from all over the area and stumbled in, not knowing what to expect. They were surprised when we would not leave, and they tried to negotiate with us. That was where Joe Wall got the idea of hanging on when they came to arrest us. I was sitting near the door, and when the police started arresting us, most people just sat there, as they had been trained. But one man reached into the mail slot and hung on for dear life.

I thought I would do that, too. So when they came for me—I was way back there—I grabbed hold of the mail slot and hung on.

The first few people walked out under their own power. Mike was the first one who had to be carried out. After his arrest, people got the idea that that was what to do.

Some people hung on. And the people who hung on to the mail slot also hung on to each other. While Joe Wall was hanging on to the slot, I hung on to him. When our hands were inside, the abortion personnel stuck us with sharp objects, probably letter openers.

There is a lot of discussion about whether to walk

or go limp or hang on. In Maryland, the rescuers set a pattern, urging people to go limp. They said that they could not leave of their own free will when people were in mortal danger. They would not resist, but they would not cooperate. They never criticized people who walked, especially since one of the walkers was Marilyn Szewczyk, an early leader, and the person who opened all the pregnancy centers. Marilyn always walked because she had arthritis, and the pain when they put her arms behind her back was excruciating. If she got bumped with her arms back there, she really suffered. So she would walk, and nobody criticized her.

I decided to hang on, to buy more time. As long as we stay at a rescue site, the babies live, and the counselors have a chance to talk to women, offering them all the help they need.

My own decision is that we can walk and chew gum. We can appeal to the consciences of the police and the community and also hang on to buy more time. And after all the discussion and negotiating, the officers who are still there probably will not have any sudden change of heart because someone is not resisting. There have been demonstrations—not rescues, demonstrations—about other causes for years, with people going limp and being hauled away. So it does not automatically touch the officer's heart. At least, I never saw that happen.

Several months later, everybody who was arrested in Paoli went to court. They were all released on a technicality. The prosecutor used the language for a misdemeanor, and the charge was just a summary offense. Apparently that was enough to invalidate the case.

St. Louis, 1986.

Tom Herlihy and I had already been convicted, though. We had been separated from everyone else after the arrests, because we were from out of state. After the arrests, we were held for about a week. Tom was at Chester county jail, and I was out at Bucks county jail.

As the police were driving Tom and me away, they were remarking on how well organized the rescue was: "You guys must plan this. That was so smooth!" We were just amateurs, and we knew it. We just looked at each other and listened to them. But they went on and on about it, about how organized it was and about how much planning it must have taken, all the brain work that went into it. Of course, maybe they were just trying to trap us into a conspiracy charge, but I do not think they were. I think they were just reacting honestly. And they were impressed.

A magistrate came into the police station, got behind a desk, and we went to trial. The Constitution guarantees the right to a speedy trial, and we got one. It took place in a very small office, and we could not get an audience in there to observe what was going on. They did not allow anybody in there. It was just the two of us and the judge. And then the cop came in and testified.

We sat down in front of the judge, and Tom read from the Bible, saying we have to obey God rather than man. He explained about the "legal necessity" defense. I sat there with him and let him do the work.

The judge listened until Tom had finished, then found us guilty and banged down his little hammer. Then he begged us to agree to pay a fine or promise to stay away from the mill, because he did not want

"We're gonna break your arm," they said, and so they did. The Rev. Dan Scalf has his elbow broken by police during a rescue at Rocky Mountain Planned Parenthood in Denver, 1986.

Man being thrown had lain down in driveway to block vehicles. Rocky Mountain Planned Parenthood, Denver, 1986.

to send us to jail. I cannot remember exactly what he was begging us to do, but whatever it was, it was not acceptable. So we went off to jail for a week, and then we were released. That was long before everybody else got off.

After that, we got started doing rescues in Bridge-port. That was where we began to build in numbers, as we did rescues week after week. Eventually, we closed the mill there. The abortionist tried to open in another community, but we found out in time and got the local residents all stirred up. They resisted and kept him out.

After that the Philadelphia people started rescues at the center of the city, at the large mill on Roosevelt Boulevard. The rescue group was growing steadily, and it was pretty lively. Some kids were arrested as well—a new generation of rescuers.

At that time, I was living with Susan in Delaware and going back to St. Louis once in a while.

Around that time, the Pro-Life Action Network, or PLAN, got started with a meeting in Appleton, Wisconsin. I was in jail at the time of the meeting, but it sounded like a good thing. The activists—sidewalk counselors and rescuers—had always had their meetings during other events, like the National Right to Life convention. So it was a significant step when they were big enough to have a national conference for themselves.

The year before there had been an activist conference in Florida, sponsored by the Debate Foundation and organized by Jean Emond and Franky Schaeffer. But nothing came of the meeting. Franky Schaeffer had a dramatic meeting of rescue leaders, and it looked as if he was getting ready to throw himself into rescuing babies. But then he just disappeared.

Franky Schaeffer wrote some good things about rescues, and he helped some people to get free of their enslavement to pseudolaws.

11 Rusted-Out Justice

A team of us went out to Pittsburgh in April 1985 to help organize a rescue there. Tom Herlihy, Joe Wall and I went. At that stage, they were just trying to set up a network of activists in the area. There was a dispute between the Pennsylvania Prolife Federation and People Concerned for the Unborn Child, or PCUC. PCUC was prepared to consider rescues seriously and had left the federation.

After the split, Mary Winter kept working to bring people together. She had the idea of organizing something prolife and profamily, including not only prolife organizations but also the Keystone Alliance, which fought pornography and other related issues. It was a kind of seamless garment. She always wanted to get involved in rescues, but her husband put his foot down: "One thing, Mary. Don't ever get arrested."

Mary had a couple of these coalition meetings every year. Joe Wall kept in touch with them. So when she had a meeting in Pittsburgh, she invited us to come up there and talk about rescues. Tom brought a videotape of the rescues in Maryland, with the singing and all the arrests. People were enthralled. They watched it and cried and said, "We have got to do that." And that's when Doris Grady said, "We're going to do it."

Members of the Pro-Life Direct Action League gather at the steps of the Supreme Court, 1985.

Doris worked out the idea of the American Abolitionist Society. That was the name they decided to use. And she started organizing for a rescue in May.

Two days before the rescue, Tom and Joe went to Pittsburgh for a final planning meeting. I did not go, and I still regret that, because there should have been some discussion about disarming the murder weapons. I wanted to ask people if they would mind if we disarmed them if we got inside. But Tom and Joe were sure that people would not be ready for that, and we should not even bring up the topic. These were new people, and this was their first rescue. Also, at the time, no one really thought we could get inside, let alone get to the weapons.

Actually, it was not exactly their first. There had been a rescue there six or seven years before, when Jeanne Miller and Lucy O'Keefe were working to get people all over the country to rescue. Juli Loesch was with them at that first rescue in Pittsburgh. But this was the first in a long time.

I thought we should at least talk about the question of disarming weapons. Looking back, I think we should have disarmed them, because we went to a very large abortion mill, and we could have shut them down. We did not achieve that, and sixty babies may have died, though I am sure some lives were saved.

The planning meeting was on Thursday. On Friday, Tom, Joe Wall and Liz Little went down to the city's largest abortion mill, Women's Health Services, to look it over. Tom and Liz posed as a couple considering abortion, and they got a general idea of the inside layout. Joe went up the fire escape to see if we could get in that way. We were not too sure how to get inside.

The doors of the fire escape were locked. And we found out later that they were locked from the inside too. So much for fire escapes.

We were afraid that they would stop us right at the elevator, and we spent a lot of time arguing about how to get in. People were describing elaborate plans, with one person going up to the fourth floor and bringing the elevator back to the third floor, and people going in by twos and threes and waiting in the restrooms for five minutes, then everybody converging on the third floor and taking charge.

Joe knew it was going to get screwed up. Finally, he said, "Look, I've seen this before. All these fancy plans get balled up. Just walk right in, and go where you want to go. If you look as if you belong there, nobody will challenge you until it is too late."

That was what they decided to do. On Saturday we just walked right past the guard at the elevator and went to the mill on the third floor. There were six killing rooms there. It was the biggest killing center not only in Pittsburgh but on the whole East Coast.

After all the worry about how to get in, with people asking us to show them how, we just knocked on the door, and the receptionist buzzed and they opened the door. We went right in, went straight to the back and opened the door. There were the killing rooms, one little room after another, a whole line of little doors.

When we opened the first door and found a killing room, everybody wanted to pile into that one little room. But there were more doors down the corridor, so we tried them, too. And everyone tried to get into the second room. It took some time to get everybody sorted out, with two or three in each room, because people were nervous. But eventually everybody got into place, and they all locked themselves in.

After a check to see that there were people in each room, that we had gotten them all, Joe and I locked ourselves in the last room. We put prolife literature all over the room and then knelt to pray the Rosary. When the police came, Joe read a plea to them not to cooperate in the killing, but they ignored it.

The abortion mill staff were just standing back, watching. Prolifers are always afraid that the staff will do something, but usually they don't. Sometimes you get a belligerent abortionist, somebody who will block you or something, but that is very rare. This was the first in years for the Pittsburgh prolifers but also for the abortionists. We forgot that sometimes.

After everyone got settled, and Joe and I finally locked ourselves in, we looked at that murder weapon. I wanted to ask the people there whether they would mind if we dismantled the weapon. But Tom and Joe had discussed it and did not want to change their decision in the middle of the action. There were lots of people there who told us later that it would have been okay with them if we had disarmed the murder weapons. We could have had a quick discussion or consultation. In her room, Juli Loesch disarmed the weapon, but nobody else did.

When the police decided to break the door down, we put the abortionist's table in their way. But they used their billy clubs to pry the door open, and after about ten minutes, they got in. They rushed in and pushed the table back. We ran and jumped on the machine, grabbed it for dear life. They kicked us and kicked us and knocked us down. That machine was

Joe Wall, after arrest, being dragged away by St. Louis County police.

battered all over the room. While they were prying us off, they threw it all over the room. They did more damage than we ever did. Between Juli and the police, two of the six weapons were put out of commission.

The police dragged us out of the room and then asked us to walk out of the building. We refused. They said they would make us pay for that, and they meant it.

They put our handcuffs on in back, then put their clubs between the links and dragged us out that way. What that did was to put all the pressure on our wrists, almost breaking them.

One officer, named O'Neill, started to pull Joe's pants off. He got them almost all the way off before he stopped. He never did explain that. He also searched Joe's pockets. When he found a Rosary, he threw it away in disgust.

Outside, the cops took Joe by the legs to drag him to the police van. His shirt slid way up, and his bare skin was on the pavement. When they got him into the police van, his whole back was bleeding and raw.

Tom Herlihy, Joe and I were not from the area, so we were separated from the rest and held for four days. Everyone else was released that day. There were thirteen people who risked arrest. Most were charged with misdemeanors or summary offenses, but Joe and I were charged with felonies. They charged us with trespass, criminal trespass (a felony), criminal mischief and resisting arrest.

In November we had a five-day trial. Our attorneys tried to raise the necessity defense, which had been used by the Berrigans and other people resisting nuclear weapons. But the judge ruled that there was no

*John Ryan (center) and members of the Pro-Life Direct
Action League on their knees on the steps of the Supreme
Court, 1985.*

"imminent danger", which is required for the defense. The abortion mill administrator testified that they killed fifty babies that day, but the judge did not see any danger in that.

The jury found us not guilty of criminal mischief and resisting arrest but guilty of defiant trespass, a misdemeanor, and criminal trespass, the felony.

The judge wanted a presentence investigation, which would take weeks to prepare. He said he would release us on $5,000 bail, with the condition that we stay away from all abortion mills. Of course we could not promise to do that, and we told him so. I asked him to sentence us right away and get it over with, but he wanted time to think.

The judge, Raymond Novak, was once a Jesuit priest. He said that he could see we were people with principles. But, he said, he had principles, too. We knew what that would mean. He spoke about the need to obey the law, regardless of our feelings about it. He said, "I have sworn to the people of this state to enforce the law, and I will do so."

You would think that some of his Jesuit training would have rubbed off, even if he left the community. But he seemed to be enslaved to the letter of the law even when it was obviously unjust. He even set aside the necessity defense in his struggle to prove his allegiance to *Roe vs. Wade*.

In the end, he locked us up. We were in jail for over two months, until finally we were released pending the outcome of an appeal.

I was in jail in Florida when we lost that appeal. They wanted me back in Pennsylvania for sentencing for the two convictions, including one felony. That was what finally got me out of Florida in October 1988, when John Broderick persuaded them to extradite me for sentencing.

12 Disarming Weapons

Joan has always acted in gray areas between non-violence and violence—hanging on, destroying weapons, refusing to cooperate. At every step, it has been easy to misunderstand her. On the face of it, actions such as hers could be motivated by love, or by anger.

Joan has shared the vulnerability of babies and pregnant women. She has chosen solidarity with them in their times of crisis. She has not shrunk from the violence that has been turned toward her, happy that it was deflected from the babies at least for a short time. She has absorbed that violence and forgiven her attackers.

And yet, some people following her may imitate her actions with a very different spirit. But there are more effective ways to accomplish the goals of an angry person. They may try to surpass her work by violence. The test of anger is: Can you destroy your enemy?

Such "imitation" is empty. Joan is motivated by love. The ultimate test of love, unchanged in two thousand years, is: Will you die for the person you love?

—jcok

The first time I got into a killing room was in 1981, shortly after Mike Reid disarmed some weapons. He did that in December 1980. A few weeks later, a group of us were at Reproductive Health Services, and we saw an opportunity to get inside. We jumped through the receptionist's little window to get in. But we did not get to the killing room, because the abortion staff locked the internal doors right away.

There was another time in Bridgeton when we got into the killing rooms. John Ryan got in one room, and I got in another. But all I did was unplug it and wrap the cord around myself so that if the police dragged me they would pull the machine over. I am a little ashamed of that feeble effort.

They had a very large number of police that day, and they knocked the door open. They dragged me away, tangled in the machine.

After that, when John said we should disarm weapons, I was always enthusiastic. And after that first time, I always tried to do it. But it was not until 1984 that I was able to do it again, at Barnes Hospital (Washington University).

In early 1984, after we had been released from the jail term for violating the injunction, John and I dismantled two murder weapons with Dave Floyd.

Whenever I use the word *murder* I have to stop and explain carefully that I am referring to what the abortionist does, not to what the woman does. Most of the time, she is a victim too, along with the child. "Murder" means killing a person with a clear understanding of what you are doing, with malice and forethought, without any compulsion. For many women, that is not what happens. A child is killed, but the woman's knowledge or freedom may be limited. So what she does should not always be called murder. But the abortionist is different. He is not emotionally distraught, and he knows exactly what he is doing. What he does is murder, and he uses the carefully crafted tools of an assassin. He uses murder weapons.

The first time was at Barnes Hospital, on Euclid Street in St. Louis, which had some association with Washington University.

Four of us—John Ryan, Dave Floyd, a counselor named Mary Anne and I—went there early in the morning. We went right up into the hospital, early in the morning so no patients would be there. We were the first ones into the waiting room. As soon as they were opened, we walked right in.

It was inside the hospital, but it was a separate unit, just like an abortion mill. It had two rooms with suction aspiration machines, right in the hospital amid everything else.

As we walked past the receptionist's desk into the abortion chambers, someone said, "You can't go back there." We went right into the chambers and locked ourselves in.

Mary Anne stayed in the waiting room, counseling the women who came in. She told them that these weapons had been disarmed and that the babies would not be killed that day. She suggested that they could take some literature, and they could go to a real pregnancy aid group or just go home for the day.

While she was talking, John and Dave and I locked ourselves in the first abortion chamber and cut the cord and the tubing. We made some errors, because we were so nervous. At first, we did not look around. We could have darted all over the place and gotten back. But we did not know there was more than one machine, and we did not look around. After we cut up the wires and tubing, John opened the window and threw the wire cutters out to another roof, and we shut the window.

Then we waited, but no one came. Finally we peeked out and went down to look around and found another killing room with no one in it. So I locked myself in there, wishing that we had looked around before we tossed the wire cutters out; however, I finally was able to pull the cord out of the back of the machine.

I stayed in that room, locked up, until the police finally came. Several times they asked us to leave. They kept asking the same thing.

We had discussed this beforehand. Should we just leave when the job was done, when the murder weapon was dismantled? We had decided against that, because we could still be a witness for any women who would come.

Eventually the police had to break down the doors to get in and get us out. They did not knock the doors off the hinges; they just rammed them open.

The police were really nice, almost timid about asking us to leave. "Would you leave? Won't you leave?" It was unusual. At first, I thought they were just hospital security guards, but then there were city police. They stayed non-brutal, but eventually they got us out.

All four of us got arrested. They took us out in wheelchairs. John was the last one out. As he was rolling down the hall, a woman asked what was going on. John told her that they were killing babies there, and that we had come to rescue them. She asked how she could get in touch with us because she wanted to join us. Later, she did call and join our group.

After we were all released, John called the newspapers and told them what we had done to the murder weapons. Then there was a fight that we just watched. Barnes Hospital said that they did not have an abortion unit, that it belonged to Washington University. Washington University said that it was not theirs—it belonged to Barnes. For the next couple of days, there were conflicting stories on the radio and in the newspapers, going back and forth about who owned the abortion mill. The case never came to trial because no one wanted to claim the abortion mill. It was great.

Before then, the only person who had disarmed murder weapons had been Mike Reid. At our rescues, we usually never got to the killing rooms, just to waiting rooms and hallway doors. After Mike did it, there was tremendous pressure in St. Louis not to disarm the weapons. They said that if anybody did it, then the whole group, even if they had not agreed to do it, or participated, would get the same more serious charges.

But we started disarming weapons at other places, too.

We had another failed attempt to disarm murder weapons at Reproductive Health Services (RHS) in 1984. We went through the receptionist's little window, but all the doors were locked. We tried to find out where the killing rooms were, but they had locked them all up ahead of us. So we just locked ourselves in another room.

There was a young fellow with us who locked himself into the ladies' room. The abortionist's staff were all in front of us, coming down a hallway toward us. They had their doors all locked, and we could not get through them. There was a door to the right, which led to their counseling room. I tried to get through to where the mothers were, but I couldn't get through the abortionist's blockade. And then a large number of clinic personnel came charging at us, and so we just went where we could—"You go left; I'll go right"—and he ended up in the ladies' room by accident.

The police had to break in to get us, and in the meantime we put literature everywhere, destroyed the birth control pills—which are also murder weapons—tearing them up and putting them in the garbage can.

The police really tried hard to make us walk. One officer put me in a wheelchair, but I kept flipping out of it. The officer squashed me down on the floor, put his knee in my back and twisted my arm, trying to persuade me to walk out.

A black pro-death counselor who was very beautiful kept saying, "Why don't you walk?" I said, "You're going to kill little babies, and I would be helping you." She really sounded very sympathetic: "Well, you're going to get hurt. Please just walk; you're going to get hurt."

In the fall of 1984, after the rescue movement got started in the Philadelphia area, we were out at Norristown, and we got into the building a couple of times. Once when I went into the building, and we were all locked up in the killing rooms, I asked for permission to disarm the weapons. I asked Mike McMonagle, who was right there, "Do you mind if I disarm this murder weapon?" and he said, "I don't mind."

Jack O'Brien was our leader, but he was not in the room, so we started dismantling the weapon. We got a little bit carried away. Not only were the murder weapons dismantled but also some other damage was done. There was some very minor damage to the wall. People did not realize that there was no need to do that. The damage did not look that bad and was barely visible.

Later, people said that the danger in a rescue is always that people may not be able to control themselves. One person told me, "I can't trust myself, so we can never do things like this if people can't trust themselves."

Of course people can trust themselves! I presume that people would only try to disarm the murder weapons. Anyone could get carried away, but that was my fault. The leadership can always keep such incidents under control, saying, "Anyone who wants to may disarm weapons, but don't touch anything else."

Our people will always follow the leadership. If somebody insists on doing something that he is not supposed to do, despite what leadership is saying, you can always block him. It is not a serious problem.

But after that, people were always asking what would happen, how we would prevent chaos, although nothing came of it in that incident. The case was no different from any of the other trespass cases.

It looked a little bit messy. There were wrappers from the instruments that had been in the autoclave and things like that. And some scratches on the wall. That is why I tell people to disarm the murder weapons, but in a way that does not look as if everything has been ransacked.

I tried to convince the rescuers that we could do this in such a way that people would not be upset about the results. For one thing, you tell people ahead of time, don't touch anything that's not used in killing children, don't leave things scattered around and when you take off the wrappings from the autoclave, put them in the garbage can.

In June 1985 we disarmed some weapons in Wilmington.

After the incident in Norristown, the prolifers kept doing rescues, but they wouldn't allow anyone to disarm weapons. They tried to get me to pledge that we would not do it, and we had a big fight over questions of conscience. Jack and I were debating all the time about whether we should require a pledge about refraining from destruction of weapons. Every meeting we got into an argument. Every single meeting ended up that way, and everyone was in turmoil, because we loved each other so much, and we were stuck with each other, but we were fighting all the time. It was just terrible.

So I said, listen, watch this rescue and see how it could be done if people will follow instructions. We had a rescue in Delaware. Jack was present but did not participate in the actual rescue, but a lot of other people did. We had about eighteen people working with us, most from Pennsylvania and a few from Delaware.

We went to the Women's Health Organization in Wilmington. We got in, and it was great. We got to all three of the killing rooms, got to the killing machines and dismantled them. We did not cut the cords this time, because Jack was so against this idea, and we wanted to show him that we could disarm the murder weapons without even doing that. We unscrewed everything, unscrewed the tubing and took it out, and dismantled everything very neatly. The disarming was all done by dismantling, not destruction. I wanted to show that if you do not want to deal with the questions raised by destruction, you can at least dismantle.

After we got the tubes out, we desterilized everything and laid it all out nice and neat. We got all the paper and put it in the garbage can. In fact, the police came in when we had that partly done. One officer handcuffed me, but then he went out, and I went back to work cleaning up the paper wrappers.

The police got photographs of the rooms and showed them in court; every room was clean and neat. You should have seen them. We totally disarmed all the murder weapons, but it all looked neat. We did this to several rooms. Everybody was instructed, and everybody kept it tidy. Everybody was doing it the right way. People were in control.

One of Jack's concerns was that if anyone did it, everyone would be charged and take the blame. He knew that I was not going to sit by—no prolifer would sit by and let another prolifer take the blame for what he did—so of course I would go into court and say I did it.

I do not think that everyone would be charged with the same thing. I do not think the prosecutor would want to hit everyone with the same charge, because he does not want a lot of people in jail. So I do not think that that is a major risk.

But I do think that the risk of extra charges could scare people off.

There is a problem when people want to ensure that no one gets any extra charges. If the rescuers are going to stand in solidarity with each other and insist on the same charge, when you have done more, that is a problem. But as long as people talk about it ahead of time, and they make clear informed choices ahead of time, it does not have to be a serious problem. It is not fair to surprise people with this. If they presume that they are going to do a rescue in a particular way, and then all of a sudden they get hit with these charges, that is not fair.

In Pennsylvania, the police could charge everybody with being part of a conspiracy, even if only one person dismantled the weapons. That bothered Jack. I agreed that if it affected numbers and hurt recruiting, that might be a reason just to block the doors inside or stay in the waiting room and not go into the killing rooms or touch anything. I thought we should try it and see if the numbers dwindled.

I thought we should just put it to people, asking them whether they would be willing to take the risk of being charged with conspiracy along with the person who disarmed the weapons. The person who does the disarming will volunteer that information before the trial, but the police and prosecutor might just ignore that and charge everybody. If people were not willing to take this risk, and you could see that it was hurting your numbers, that could be a good reason not to disarm weapons.

What I did not understand was the way people were drawing conclusions that were not grounded in facts and getting nervous over mere speculation. The main concern was that it would hurt our numbers, and we did not know that it would. In Philadelphia, they were big on numbers, because Norristown brought out our biggest numbers at that time, with sixty-four arrests. (Gaithersburg had been bigger, with 140 risking arrest, but only four people actually got arrested because the killing was canceled. Norristown set the record for that time for the number of actual arrests.)

At that rescue the police got very violent. The group had stayed back by the street, not blocking women as they went in, planning instead to block the abortionist when he came. It was hard for people to watch women going in and not block the doors, and everybody was tense. And then the police snuck the abortionist through the building next door, so that when he stepped out into the open, he had only a few feet to run to get in the door of his mill.

When he did that, people were really angry, and they charged the door. For a minute, there was an uncontrolled mob. People were banging on the doors, and the police were no help. They got rough immediately, and they accidentally threw me against a glass door, which shattered. So there were screaming and shouting and banging and glass breaking, and then everybody heard that someone had been cut and there was a little blood by the door. It was hard for the leaders to regain control, but they managed.

After that, there was a lot of discussion about controlling emotions. There were some heated arguments. When you are arguing among people you really love and respect, you feel so frustrated. That was a very painful period, in Philadelphia.

The Delaware action went beautifully, though, and in court I said I had disarmed the weapons.

The next time we disarmed a weapon was in Washington, during the 1986 March for Life. In 1986 we had a pray-in on the Supreme Court steps for the first time. In 1986, rescue teams from all over the country went to different abortion mills in the city of Washington, trying to make the city abortion free during the march. The St. Louis group went to the abortion mill near the Catholic University, almost in the shadow of the National Shrine. That is where the worst atrocities in the city occur, with the largest babies killed. Of course, smaller babies are just as precious, but the late abortions include longer torturing of the baby, and everybody who is involved knows what is going on. With early abortions, some of the staff may be honestly ignorant, but not with late abortions. They are so blatant, so brutal, so obvious.

The Philadelphia people were also at a mill in Washington, but I went with the St. Louis people, because I did not get a chance to see them very often. There were sixteen or seventeen of us, and we disarmed everything in that place, all the murder weapons. The abortion mill attached to the hospital was very distinct from the rest of the hospital, even more clearly delineated than the unit at Barnes Hospital, where the abortion mill was deep inside the hospital. This was in a separate building on the hospital grounds.

We disarmed everything that was used for killing. We opened up the packages of instruments that had been sterilized, and we desterilized them. We cut the cords and ripped them out of all the machines used in the killing.

John Ryan always seems to get hurt, and he got it here, too. The police really hurt him. They had to break into the room; we had things up against the door. After they had broken in, they dragged us out through the office and waiting room, where we had somebody who was counseling.

Outside the office, they took us down a hall and around a corner. After they dropped me in the hallway, I heard John crying out, and I heard somebody say, "Stop hurting him!"

He was in the elevator. They had him up and they were choking him, twisting his arms.

A friend who shall remain nameless pulled the fire alarm—the phantom rescuer, wandering around doing little things to prevent killing. So there was a tremendous racket there, with the fire alarm and the screaming.

We got a fifty-dollar fine for that rescue, which we never paid.

13 Pensacolski

The long confrontation in Florida started when I asked John Burt if I could come there to help organize a rescue team. I had been hearing about John Burt for a couple of years. He was a media focus for a while, because he strengthened the stereotype that the pro-abortion media wanted us to have. He had formerly been a member of the Ku Klux Klan, and now he was a completely converted Christian and a prolifer. That made a lot of dishonest reporters think he was the man to interview, since they could distort the truth about this good man.

Because John Burt was always being attacked, pro-lifers wanted to know who he was. He was a member of the Klan before he became a Christian. But he left all that behind. And after he became a Christian, he went to work to help women. He opened Our Father's House, a shelter for pregnant women.

On Christmas 1984, there were some bombings in Pensacola. Three abortion mills were destroyed. John Burt was a prime target of investigations, of course. When Matt Goldsby and Jimmy Simmons were arrested and put on trial, John Burt supported them, although he had not been involved.

I was at Earl Appleby's office one day when John Burt called. I asked Earl, when he was through talking,

to give the phone to me, and I introduced myself to
John Burt. I told him I was involved in the rescue
movement, and I was wondering if he would mind if
I came down to give a talk and to get together a little
group of activists. Then maybe after the talk, we could
organize a rescue. We could invite those who were
interested to join us.

He thought it was a great idea. I told him that I
had a trial coming up in Maryland, for disarming some
murder weapons at the Planned Parenthood mill in
Annapolis, and I might end up in jail for a little while
with that, so I wanted to come to Pensacola soon. He
said that would be fine.

He called me back a week later to say the rescue
was all set for March 26.

In the meantime, we got a little group together.
Several people agreed to come down to help, includ-
ing John Haring, Earl Appleby, John Ryan and Joe
Scheidler.

We gave a talk at a church there. Not many people
attended.

There were a few proabortion picketers outside. A
couple of women were trying to pretend they were
nuns. They had probably been to a costume store.
They had habits on, but no stockings. They were wearing little white slippers, and their legs were bare. I
pointed out to the newsmen that these were fake nuns,
that they were out of habit. They were not amused or
even interested; they wanted to know about the born-
again ex-Klansman and his ties to the Christmas
bombers.

It always amazes me that the abortionists get
away with portraying themselves as progressives or

liberals. I have never heard anyone associated with Planned Parenthood apologize for the open racism of their founder, Margaret Sanger. She wanted to segregate and sterilize "subhumans". She talked about strategies for keeping "rebellious" blacks in line. She was disgusted with charity programs that made life easier for people who, she thought, would be better off dead. And although she and her friends have hidden themselves behind a lot of propaganda about "choice", they praised the Nazis for their "efficient" eugenics policies in the 1930s, and today they praise the "efficient" Chinese for their coercive policies. Amazing or not, they do get away with it, and the newsmen in Pensacola just wanted to talk about the KKK and bombs.

The number of proabortion picketers outside was about as large as the number of prolifers inside. It was a very small showing. But we each spoke. Penny Lea was there, and she spoke, too. And we announced that we were going to do a rescue.

John Ryan was not able to join us in the rescue, because he was running the Pro-Life Direct Action League and could not take a chance on being in jail out of state. And Joe Scheidler was going to be a part of the support group. I was the only out-of-towner who was going to do the rescue. We did not know how many local people would agree to join.

When we asked for volunteers that evening, we found there were going to be John Burt and his daughter and two other women from the shelter who were born-again Christians. So there were just five of us.

But the next morning there were lots of picketers,

over a hundred, maybe two hundred. It was packed. The picketers were great.

Later, after I was in jail awaiting trial, we got really bad publicity; we lost all that support. Apparently they all decided that rescue missions were really radical. They all got scared and apologized to the rest of the community. It was almost as if a bombing had taken place. They all said they were sorry, and they said they did not know all those horrible out-of-town people. All the picketers suddenly disappeared. It was funny—after the rescue, the activists in Pensacola had hardly any support at all.

That morning, when we arrived at the site, John had the clippers for the murder weapons in his pocket, but he never got into a killing room. We could not get in the front door; the abortion staff and the police were there waiting for us; and everything was locked. Out in the parking lot, there were a lot of police, and there were a lot of prolife picketers out front. John Ryan had the bullhorn, Joe Scheidler's trademark.

The NOW woman, Georgia, said I pushed her when I was going in. That was interesting, because when she gave her first deposition to the police, she said I had never touched her. It was only later that she said I did. After I gave my testimony and about ten ministers gave theirs, all saying that I never touched her when I was going in, she changed it a little, and she said I brushed her as I went in. The judge said he did not know whether I brushed her or not, but evidently if I did it was just an accident, and the assault charges were dropped.

When I saw we could not get in the front door, I led the way around the back of the building. We went up a ramp to the side door. I tried the door, but it was locked.

As I knocked and stepped back, the NOW woman opened the door and came out, talking with some man. She swung the door wide open while she stood there talking to him. I went in right past them. They were standing away from the door, and I did not go within two feet of them.

Inside, I started to run up the stairs, and that was when Linda Taggart, the mill administrator, showed up. I saw her out of the corner of my eye, and I started up the stairs. She said, "You can't go up there!"

I did not say anything; I just kept going on up.

We suspected the killing rooms were upstairs; we did not know for sure. We knew that if we got there early enough, we could be there before the abortionist was a threat to the babies and the women. Some women had already gone to the waiting room, going in the front door and turning left into the waiting room.

A prolife Filipino girl had gone in and handed out some literature. When she came out, we went in. She went in the regular way, through the front door; she must have had an appointment.

As I went up the stairs, Karissa Epperly and Sarah Burt started to follow me. John Burt, the last one through the door, had been talking to a police-man. When he saw us go in, he turned and hustled after us.

Mary blocked the door from the outside. She was not able to get inside before the police or abortion workers shut the doors and locked them, so she sat there alone and blocked the door. She was arrested, but she got out on probation after she spent a few days in jail.

When this all came to trial, John Burt was convicted of assault. He was accused of running through the door behind us, grabbing Linda Taggart, knocking her against the wall, picking her up and knocking her against the other wall and then running up the stairs—all with a policeman right behind him. They had been talking together when John saw that we were going in and ran after us. The officer went right after John and lost sight of him for a split second when John turned a corner ahead of him. In that split second, he supposedly committed two assaults. Fast worker!

The officer testified that he was right behind John, and he did not see anybody before he went up the stairs. But John was convicted anyway. Incredible.

There was another officer who eventually refused to testify against me. That was interesting.

But anyway, that morning, I went into the killing chamber at the top of the stairs, closed the door and tried to lock it. There was only one machine in the room, no sterile setups. There was no autoclave, just one suction aspiration machine. I unplugged it, and I tried to rip the cord out of the back of the machine. I yanked and yanked on it. I put my feet up against it, yanking with all my strength, but the cord would not come out. Then the police got the door open and grabbed me.

The first officer could not get me off. So he left and got a second officer, and the two of them came in and worked on my hands, prying my fingers off one at a time. As soon as they got me off, I went limp. They thought I was going to struggle, because I had been holding so tightly to the machine. So they held me down, with a knee on my back, handcuffed me and dragged me out into the hallway. Then they went after Sarah Burt and Karissa Epperly, who were in another killing room.

John Burt had run upstairs and looked in the other two rooms, but they were not killing rooms. The police grabbed him and handcuffed him on the floor in the hallway.

The girls were still working away. They had put their machine up against the door, and the police could not get in. They were banging on the door, but Sarah and Karissa kept on working. They shredded the electrical cords and the tubing and dumped the chemicals on the floor. They did a good job. They took care of that room very well. It looked as if I were the amateur, while they accomplished what they set out to do in their room.

Finally the police got the door open, grabbed them and handcuffed them. But while they were doing that, I got up and went back into my room. I pushed the machine over with my shoulder. When the police heard the crash, they came running back into my room and dragged me out again, and threw me on top of John Burt.

While I was crashing that machine, one officer had already dragged one of the girls out and thrown her on top of John, who was lying flat on the floor. They got the last of us and threw her on the heap, too. There were three women on top of John.

We rolled off him, because we could see that he could not breathe. He was choking and gasping. But as we rolled off him, the police would throw us back on. We would roll off, and they would throw us back on. We kept saying that we were not trying to escape, it was just that he could not breathe. That went on for a while until finally one officer realized what was going on. John's face was blood red, and he was gasping, so they let us roll off and stay off. Then we sat there singing hymns and praying. John just lay there for a while, trying to get his breath back.

I sang "Father, We Adore You" and "Give Life a Chance". The girls prayed in tongues.

A few officers checked the women and did a body search. Then an officer wearing a helmet and jackboots—a motorcycle cop, evidently—came stomping up. He was a tough guy. He got his billy club out and jabbed John in the side. John was just lying there, flat on the floor. The policeman jabbed him on one side with his billy club and searched his pockets, then jabbed him in the other side and searched some more. There was no reason for that, and we protested: "What are you doing? He's not struggling; he's not resisting; he's just lying there."

Then we all got carried out and thrown in the police car. They took us down to the station and held us. A huge bond was placed on each of us—$20,000 or something like that.

This was the first rescue and first arrest for the girls, and they were upset, especially Karissa. She had a little baby, and was worried about him.

John Haring, the lawyer, was arrested on the parking lot. He stepped on to the parking lot to talk to a policeman. The officer told him that he had better get going. But as he was walking off, they arrested him.

A lawyer, talking to an officer on the parking lot: one serious crime. He got six months' probation for it.

But anyway, John Haring was having a hard time while we were in jail. He really wanted us out of jail and put up the cash to get Karissa out. Karissa had a "failure to thrive" baby, a cute little boy named Jonathan, just six months old, who was in and out of the hospital constantly.

John Burt got out first. Some ministers got him out. Sarah was next; then after a couple of days Karissa got out. I was in four days.

I left Florida and came back a month later for a hearing on the sixteenth. At the hearing, the prosecutor asked the judge to make it a condition of the bond that we stay away from the abortion mill. The judge refused to do so and specifically said that we were not ordered to stay away from there. But he warned us against any "incidents". He said that if he heard of an incident, he would revoke the bond.

To me—and to any intelligent human being—"incident" meant something like creating a ruckus or doing something that incurs an arrest. So we did not worry about going back out there to picket the place.

Sarah went home with her father. But Karissa and another girl—a mother of two wonderful kids, twins— and I went over to the mill to picket for a while. We were there for about an hour, and we never once even looked at the mill, although Linda Taggart was yelling at us and taking pictures and harassing us. We kept our eyes averted, prayed and walked back and forth. We took turns with the two kids and the signs.

There was a policeman sitting in his car across the street. He never arrested us or gave us warning, never even got out of his car. He did not see any "incident".

When we were finished picketing, we got in the car and drove away. I went to St. Louis for the PLAN convention there and got arrested on April 19 in St. Louis at 7:00 in the morning. That was my last day of freedom until October 18, 1988.

When we were arrested in St. Louis, I was held for five days, because I had five outstanding warrants on me there for cases I had not taken care of. I sat in jail waiting for trial. But then on April 24, I found out my property bond was revoked in Florida because of the picketing, and that I had to be back in Florida the next day or the people who had put up my bond would jeopardize their property. Anyway, that was what I was told by the lawyer. I said I thought you could never lose a property bond if you were being held in jail somewhere else. But the lawyer said I was wrong about that and that the people who had put up a property bond for me could lose their house.

That made me think that I would never trust a compromise again. I decided that I would never again accept even a property bond. Then I learned that for me to get out of jail in St. Louis so I could go to Florida, someone would have to put up a $1,300 cash bond.

I had compromised in accepting one bond, and here was another! It put me in a bad position. In St. Louis, we had always accepted property bonds, because we always got out and it never cost us a penny. I had never expected something like this to come up. I was used to accepting property bonds. And I did not think the bond could be confiscated if I was in jail elsewhere.

I still do not know the truth of it. Lawyers can get desperate when they want you to do something—my lawyer told me that the court could confiscate the property. Later, I was told No, that was wrong, they could never confiscate it if I was in custody elsewhere.

Anyway, I accepted the $1,300 bond. That money was tied up until the spring of 1988. I got out about midnight and stayed that night with Ann O'Brien. The next day I headed for Florida. I got into the bus station in Pensacola around 1:00 in the morning and walked to John Burt's house. I stayed up to finish some letters, thinking that they should go out even if I ended up in jail.

At 9:00, we went to court, and by 9:30 we were incarcerated. The bond revocation was upheld. That came as a shock.

The judge was very angry that we had gone back to the mill and asked how we had dared to go against what he said. We told the judge that we had just picketed, that all the pictures Linda Taggart took of us showed us picketing. Not one of them showed us speaking to her or yelling at her or even looking at her. Our faces were always down, praying and holding the babies with the signs. That was all she could produce as incriminating evidence.

The judge said that he would not allow us to harass these people and said he had warned us against doing this. I said, "Judge, you said an 'incident'. We did not create any 'incident'. You told the prosecutor that you would not make it a condition of bond that we could not go there. So you're now revoking the bond for no reason."

Our lawyer, Steve Flynn, tried to say the same

thing, that it was not a condition of bond, but the judge would not listen. He revoked the bond, and we were in jail half an hour after we showed up in court.

The judge was Catholic.

The judge in Baltimore, who was the first to put me in jail, was a fallen-away Catholic. The judge who issued the injunction at Martin Luther King's old seminary and jailed Miriam and me was a deacon who went to Mass every day. The judge who jailed Joe Wall and me in Pittsburgh was an "ex"-priest. The judge in St. Louis who locked up Samuel, Ann, John and me was a devout Catholic.

It is hard to understand the extent of Catholic involvement in abortion. But when we go into court and get a Catholic judge, usually we expect the worst. The judge will probably lean over backward to prove that his legal decisions are not influenced by his "sectarian beliefs". To prove it, he will nail us. Over and over, Catholic judges insist all through a trial that abortion is not the issue, that the issue is just trespass or whatever. "I do not want to hear your philosophy or any emotional feelings", they all say. But then when the trial is over, and they have spent all that time telling us to be quiet about abortion, it comes time for sentencing. And all of a sudden, the issue is "privacy" or "pluralism" or "the American way" or some other philosophical, emotion-laden concept. In the sentence, abortion is the issue again, and it is an important issue, and the judges express their strongly held views by locking us up for as long as they can. With Catholic judges, we are tried for trespass, but we get sentenced for treason, bigotry, abusing women, everything.

When we go into court and get a Jewish judge, we

breathe a sigh of relief. Like the Catholic, he will probably tell us immediately that he is not interested in
abortion, only in trespass. But he will stick to that
when it comes time for sentencing and will give
us the same sentence he gives other convicted trespassers.

Before the trial, the case was transferred to another
judge, William Anderson. Anderson was not another
in the line of Catholics who had learned to divorce
their Faith from their lives. But sadly he was a Christian whose actions were not grounded on his faith.

Anderson held another hearing on the bond, but he
too decided to hold us in prison until the trial. Then
after the trial, during my appeal (which we lost), he
still refused to release me on bond.

The decision to hold us in jail for picketing within
the borders of the United States (without revoking
the First Amendment by normal legal procedures) had
nothing to do with the law. It was a political decision.
The attorney general of Florida said that he understood they were making a mountain out of a molehill
but that the political pressure to keep me in jail was
unbelievable. To justify keeping me in jail, they talked
about the mass killer Ted Bundy, another "repeat
offender".

While we were in jail in northern Florida, at Escambia county jail, Mary and Karissa overheard guards
talking about "accidents", about how someone was
going to find us dead. Several officers in Pensacola
did that, trying to terrify us by talking about their
plans for us.

Friends outside the jail were worried about the
death threats that we were getting, but inside we

were not too worried. It was important to protest them, and I am grateful to the people who started writing to the governor, the bishop, the city officials, the jail officials. But we were not really expecting to get killed. The police make so many threats like that at the abortion mills.

Still, the city was very hostile, and it is best to be careful. Things can happen. A person can be set up very easily. Later, I saw what can happen in a system as brutal as a maximum security prison. Things do happen, and they happen often enough that one has to be very careful. One has to be aware of what goes on around him, not jumping to conclusions, but not being naïve either.

One could be set up by anyone in the prison system, by guards or by a higher authority. A guard could just drop a hint to some crazy prisoner that a certain person had snitched on her.

Later, in Broward, I met a crazy lady who wanted to kill me. If she had gotten a chance, I believe she would have done it. I knew I had to be very careful around her and be sure that I watched for her at all times, because she was criminally insane. Her driving force was vengeance. And she thought I had snitched on her.

Sometimes you can get the idea that this is the twentieth century and we are all civilized now. When I was growing up, it was awfully hard for me to believe that such a thing as a war could ever take place again. When fighting did break out, in Lebanon, for example, I was shocked. How could people still fight in this modern age?

That was very naïve. The truth is that there are

wars—and people do get hurt in prisons. Usually it is not serious; a little violence breaks out, and there are fistfights, with everyone hollering. Probably nobody is going to sneak into your cell in the middle of the night and stab you. But you can get hurt. You can get set up. There are angry, hurting and sometimes crazy people in there.

Jail is the test of our resolve to protect babies. If the price for solidarity with the unborn is time in jail, will we still act to protect them?

The rescue, the trial and jail are parts of a single whole. Going to court and going to jail are not our ideas, but we should not be surprised or resentful about them.

Think about the women we talk to at the abortion mills. If they listen to us and do the right thing, then they are pregnant for another six or seven months. Many women find that a time of joy, but some women think pregnancy is like jail. Their decision to act in love and to give birth to a child carries a high price. For them, walking away from the abortion mill means some very specific things about their future. Why should we be surprised or resentful if the same thing happens to us?

Sometimes I think that the Lord saw his decision to give himself to his disciples, his trial and death and his time in the tomb as three parts of one event. Of course, that is the way the Church celebrates the "Triduum". But Jesus had said that he would spend three days and three nights in the tomb. Sometimes I think that maybe he meant that he was already a dead man when he got arrested on Thursday night, or even when he gave his Body and Blood to the apostles at the Last Supper.

Being the paschal Lamb for the Passover meal and being a servant who poured out his life for some fishermen, tax collectors and prostitutes were part of his death. Serving the apostles, washing their feet and giving himself to them as a sacrificial meal were not separate from his crucifixion eighteen hours later.

At the mills, we try to protect the babies. Later, we may be punished for that. We should not be surprised by that or resentful of it. It is unjust, and we can try to avoid it. But if our acts of love require that we pay a price, we should not draw back. The act of love and the sacrifice that it requires later are pieces of a single event.

American jails are barbaric. The original Quaker theory that led this nation to adopt prisons instead of corporal punishment or banishment or some other penal system was that time alone in quiet with a Bible to read would lead to inner conversion. It never worked very well, except maybe with some white-collar criminals like the Watergate people. Most of the time, nobody is even trying to make it work. Jail is just a waste of the convict's time.

Most of the punishment is being cut off from friends. But in many cases jailers see imprisonment not as a punishment in itself but as a way to put convicts in their hands, where the real punishment can begin.

When you listen to cops and judges, you begin to see that in their minds, the real deterrent built into the American judicial system is the threat of homosexual rape. That threat is never made official, but it is the real core of the prison system in this once-civilized nation. Beginning with the police at the abortuary, through the court officials including the judges, to the jailers, everyone who is entrusted with enforcing the law in America uses the threat of homosexual rape. None of them will take any responsibility for it; they all pretend to hate it. Some of them say they oppose it, and some of them are probably sincere. But all of them, at every step of the way, betray themselves at one point or another when they see your determination. The cops on the street are likely to be blunt: "Do you want to get raped in jail?" The judges will probably talk all around it: "Our system is not designed for people like you. Do you understand the grave risks you are taking?" But it is code. All of them use this barbaric threat. For them, the bottom-line deterrent is not time away from family or days without sunshine or wasted time. When a prolifer refuses to obey the illegal and immoral orders of the proabortion system, their power is threatened, and they start talking about the real basis of their power: homosexual rape.

Fortunately, the inmates are almost always far more civilized than the cops and judges and guards. The inmates have almost always been protective of prolifers and Christians who fall into their midst.

Jail time is a good time to pray. It is an opportunity for meditation and contemplation. But it is also a good time for asking God for the things we need, a good time for intercessory prayer. The Lord draws near to the poor and listens to their prayers. There are advantages to being poor.

We were in jail until the trial on July 25, 1986. I had decided to go before a judge, because I thought that juries were so weak. They just do whatever the judge says, and yet they do not know the technical details that they could use to get you off if they know the trial is a farce.

Pensacola is proabortion. At our trial, we wanted the testimony of a woman reporter who had been at the mill that morning, who had seen us knock on the front door and could testify that we had not beaten anybody up. Courts always want objective witnesses. Here was a witness who was not a prolifer and was not an abortion mill employee. We subpoenaed her as a witness.

Just before the trial we went before the judge for a conference at the bench. The reporter was there, with her boss. He argued that he did not want any of his reporters to have to testify. And she said that she did not want to testify.

Our lawyer argued that reporters could sometimes avoid testifying when they were protecting confidential sources, but this was not a matter of confidentiality. She was just going to be asked what she saw, just as if she had been walking down the street when a burglary occurred. Like any other citizen, she had a duty to testify in court about what she saw.

The judge ruled against us.

The reporter's paper had an obvious proabortion stance, but we just wanted her to testify about what she saw. She could have told the judge that we did not beat anybody up, that we were not violent. But the judge excused her and would not listen to the testimony of an unbiased reporter.

There we were, facing these huge charges, and this reporter knew what had happened. But we were denied that eyewitness.

How mean can one be? How unjust can one be? I

couldn't do that to a dog. All we wanted her to do was tell the truth about what she observed. And the head of the paper came out himself to make sure his reporter did not have to testify.

Anyway, we lost that one.

I was planning to defend myself up until the day before the trial. Then I talked to Earl Essex, who was very upset. He said that if I lost the case, it would be the first big case we had ever lost. He reminded me that there was a racketeering trial in Pennsylvania, and I was a defendant in that case. (Abortionists have used several amazing laws to go after rescuers, including antitrust laws, RICO (racketeering) laws and conspiracy charges. Their tactics were desperate, but still they cost us a lot of time and money. Right then, Pennsylvania rescuers were being charged under the laws that were written to break up the Mob.)

Earl argued that if one of the RICO defendants was convicted of a felony, that would put everybody else in some jeopardy. They could use it against all the other defendants. He said that if I had a lawyer, he could make all kinds of technical points, and then even if I lost they could appeal. But if I defended myself, I would not know what technical points to raise and that would not only mean I was more likely to lose but also that the appeal would be ruined. So the day before the trial, I agreed to have a lawyer represent me. We went to trial the next day.

During our trials, we have to maintain two principles and have our lawyers maintain them also. Number one, do what is best for the babies at our trial, not what is best for the individual defendant. Do whatever is best for the movement, for the babies.

Protecting the individual defendant is good, and it has an impact on the movement, but it is secondary. If people are afraid that they will be abandoned, that may make it hard to recruit more people for rescues. But whatever happens at our trials, it should be planned to make sure the rescues continue. The dignity of children should be upheld, the dignity that leads us to rescue.

Number two, be loyal to other rescuers. We do not ever do anything to help ourselves that might hurt another rescuer.

My lawyer knew that there were some charges of assault, so he asked a witness during cross-examination about the charges, and he suggested that it was really John Burt, not me, who had been at fault.

I got really upset with the lawyer over that suggestion, and I fired him. I could not believe that he had done something like that. I did not want to make it obvious to anyone else that he had said something damaging—I did not want to draw any more attention to it. But that never should have happened. He's a good man, but he didn't understand.

A lawyer's mentality, his professional training, is geared toward defending his client. He said that it did not matter what we said about John Burt in my trial; what we said would not necessarily hurt John in his case and could not be used against him. What a defense attorney said in one trial would not be carried over into another trial.

But I was adamant that I did not want our people making negative remarks about each other on the record. John Burt could end up before the same judge, and the judge would not be able to set aside everything he had heard, regardless of the theory that he should. Every little piece of criticism adds up.

I told the lawyer that he was breaking one of our principles and aiding a hostile witness to lie about another prolifer by criticizing John Burt and that that was intolerable. In the end, he said he would not make that mistake again, and I reinstated him.

He was just a regular lawyer who stumbled into the case as a volunteer. He was handling a legal matter for one of the girls at Our Father's House, and he happened to knock on the door when John was getting ready for the trial. John asked if he could help out with my trial, and he agreed to do so. That was really very generous. But he did not know any of the principles of our work. We tried to drum it all into him, but we are not typical criminal defendants. I really feel for him. He was very generous, but he sometimes caused harm for us because he did not understand us.

Later, after the trial, prolifers picketed Judge Anderson's house. That was not my idea, but I was very glad about it. This misguided lawyer, however, told people that I was upset about the picketing, that I was against it. It happened around Thanksgiving, but I did not hear about that until Christmas Eve. All during that time, people were holding off, because they thought I was against it. Also, people thought that if he had not been there, there would be no chance I could get out on appeal. It was really a bad, bad time all around.

It was true that I felt no personal animosity toward Anderson. He interpreted that to mean I would be against picketing his home. But I was completely in favor of picketing his home. We have to be able to

show our brother he is in the wrong. If someone does
something wrong and he does not understand what
he did, but you do, then you have a responsibility to
show him why he was wrong. He may not listen, but
you still have a responsibility to try.

The response of the bishop of Pensacola, Bishop
Keith Symons, was harmful. He told everyone that
Pensacola was a peaceful community, that he did not
like having people like me there. When he got questions about the death threats in jail, he defended the
police and guards without making any effort to find
out whether the complaints were true.

Pensacola is not a peaceful community. They kill
babies there. No community in this country is peaceful. There is hardly a spot in this country that is
free of the blood of innocent little babies. It was
brutal to dismiss these children. The threats to
prolifers were not world-class atrocities, but what
he said was an attack on the dignity of the children. As thousands of babies are torn to shreds,
the bishop announced to all the world that Pensacola was a peaceful, good community. That was just
shocking.

Later, when I was in Broward, the archbishop of
Miami was criticized because he did not give me much
support. I do not think that it is fair to criticize a busy
bishop for the things he does not get around to. I would
have liked to go to Mass there. But to be fair, it does
not make sense to criticize the bishop because one
person in prison cannot get to Mass.

Bishop Symons, however, implied that killing off
children at the rate of one in three was not disrup-
tive of the peace of his little community. He was not

bothered about it, and neither were any of his friends. That was very wrong on his part.

Bishop Symons was not alone. Later, another Catholic official, Thomas Horkan, also said things that undermined the dignity of children and undermined what we were doing to protect them. Horkan is not a bishop; he is an official of the Florida Catholic Conference. In response to questions about me, he wrote a memo to the bishops that parroted the lies told by the abortionists in Pensacola. He probably did not call the abortionists himself; he just repeated the lies that appeared in the newspapers. But even if he was just remissive, he should not have done that. He said things that were totally against Catholic teaching, ignoring the long Tradition of social thought. It was very bizarre, reading about a Catholic spokesman who was ready to treat these children as things or as an "issue". I believe he did not mean to do this, but this was indeed the result of his position, his rhetoric.

14 Noncooperation

Judge Anderson eventually got around to sentencing me. I told him I would keep on rescuing babies, and it seems he decided that he had to make sure that everyone understood clearly that the law is more important than life. In a pagan society, people do not always understand what "idolatry" is, and that was idolatry. He decided that everyone had to bow down to an idol, the law, not to God, who comes to dwell in each human heart.

The judge gave me a five-year sentence. I understand that on the same day, in the same courtroom, he sentenced two men who had been convicted of being accomplices to murder—and gave them four years each.

I had decided on noncooperation. When he sentenced me, I explained that the only way I could still work to protect babies was to resist the unjust legal system. I sat down and refused to walk. They had to carry me off to jail.

After I was sentenced, Susan and I were talking, and she asked me how it felt. I said I felt shocked at first, as if I had had a mild heart attack. But then I felt peace about it. That story got a little distorted. When I got out of jail, someone came up to me and said that she had been touched when she read that I saw all the babies all around me. The story appeared in the book of prison letters. But in fact, I did not see babies all over the courtroom or feel them.

I have had only had one spiritual experience where I felt anything like that. When my grandmother died, I felt her in the room. It seemed to me that she was very upset because she felt we were not praying for her. She was right; we were not, or I was not, anyway. I was not praying for her, because I assumed that she was in heaven. She was such a holy woman, and I thought I did not need to pray for her. But my grandmother was very upset and hurt about that. I could feel her hurt.

I believe that what I felt really happened, because Susan and I felt the same thing, and we were not in the room at the same time. And Miriam also had a dream that night about my grandmother crying because we were not constantly and fervently praying for her.

In Miriam's dream, my grandmother looked happy, but then she turned around, and Miriam realized that her face was the devil's face. Miriam said, "You're not Ganger; you're the devil. You're just trying to fool us, so we'll think that Ganger doesn't want us to pray for her."

Miriam was eleven then, and came up with this on her own. None of us had talked to each other about it before these things happened. So I believe it really happened that my grandmother was trying to communicate something to us.

But that was the only experience like that I have ever had. I did not feel babies in the courtroom when I was sentenced. What I said was misunderstood, and communication back and forth with a prisoner is so slow that the story was all over the place before I could straighten it out.

What really happened was that I said to Susan, "Can you imagine all those little babies who have been killed? They die, and no one's at their death camps. Can you imagine how they must feel if someone does try to stand up for them? We can't betray them. We can't say that we won't rescue them, because that would offend their dignity. I love these babies." I said that when I thought about the babies, it made me feel good about what was happening, even when the judge found me guilty and sentenced me to five years in jail. I painted an imaginary picture to explain how I felt, but Susan thought I was describing what I saw.

I wrote about solidarity with the babies before my sentencing. During my time in jail waiting for the trial, I became more and more convinced that we should not cooperate while we were in jail, wherever we were sent after sentencing.

Now, more and more rescue leaders are using non-cooperation as a bargaining chip. They and their people will not cooperate until they get what they want, such as the same charges to protect certain people from receiving selective prosecution, or something like that. I think that is a great idea.

I slowly came to the firm conviction that once you are sentenced, you should not cooperate. Cooperation at that point is like bowing to the sentence, assenting to the idea that you should be punished for saving lives. I had decided that even if I were given thirty days, I was not going to cooperate. I had been thinking about that for weeks before I was sentenced to five years by Judge Anderson. That was not a spur-of-the-moment decision; it was on my mind before I went into court. Nor was it a response to the five-year sentence.

I had not refused to cooperate before while I waited for five months before I was sentenced, but it was on my mind. As I thought and prayed about it, the idea grew until finally I was convinced in my heart that I would not cooperate. We in the rescue movement had been cooperating all this time. I decided then that I just could not cooperate, regardless of how much time I was sentenced.

I was told early on that if I did not cooperate, I would spend more time in jail. Usually, a large portion of a person's sentence is set aside if he is a good prisoner, who does not make any trouble or get in fights or anything. This time taken off the sentence is called "good time". If he does not cooperate, he does not get any of this good time. But that was all part and parcel of sharing the vulnerability of the babies.

Of course, the scriptural precedents teaching us how to respond are clear on the point of conviction and arrest and imprisonment. There are clear examples that we can imitate. So some people ask why I decided not to cooperate, when the Lord cooperated with his executioners.

But Jesus did not cooperate with evil. For one thing, he was silent. That is a serious form of noncooperation. If somebody asks you a question and you are silent, that is big-time noncooperation. People can think that you are being rude when they ask you a question, especially when an authority asks you a question, and you refuse to answer. That could be seen as rudeness. And certainly it is noncooperation with authority.

When Jesus walked to his crucifixion, he was obedient to his Father. He was dying for our sins. Dying like that has to do with not cooperating with evil. He was overcoming evil, abandoning himself to save all mankind. He did what he was supposed to do. In other words, he did what the Father wanted him to do.

Whatever we do, we should follow God's will. I think that Jesus would not cooperate with authorities in the midst of mass murder. If he were thrown in the prison system for saving lives or for refusing to assent to evil, he would not go along with it and support that system by making it easier. I think he would totally refuse to cooperate.

When you start to relent, start to make small concessions to the system, even tiny decisions, the system seizes on them and puts pressure on you to keep compromising. That is not paranoia; that is just a description of how the prison system works. Guards report to each other what inmates do and what is effective in keeping them in line. So if you decide that you will be a burden, then you have to stick to it and be a burden.

If you are isolated, the guards may think that they can handle you without making any concessions. But when other people begin to imitate your example, then the system has to take that into account.

Noncooperation is catching on. And it is important that the guards understand that you will do what you say you will do; if you say you will not cooperate, that means that they will definitely have a huge new burden on the system. If people compromise, though, then

the guards will think that we are not serious. They
will think that if they beg you enough, you will change.
They have to see that if you are noncooperative, then
when they go to move you, all of a sudden it will be
as if there is no bone in your body and you will be like
just skin and limp muscle. And nothing they can say
or do will change that.

Noncooperation has two very different results.
First, it helps you learn to identify with the helpless
babies. But also, more immediately, it may have a
more tangible result: it may open up the gates of the
prison for the release of large numbers of rescuers.

Some people are very hesitant about noncooperation
in jail out of concern for the jailers. You can make a
distinction between the jailers and the police officer
who is actually at the mill, right there safeguarding
the suction machine. Whatever his private thoughts
and understanding, it remains the cold truth that if
he removes you, he is clearing the way for the abortionist and babies will die. The police officer's situation
is poorly understood, but still it is clear: he is the
hired tool for the abortionist—a tool without which
the dirty work of mass killing cannot take place.

The jailer, however, is at the other end of the penal
system, and he does not necessarily know why you
are in jail. He may know what happened at the abortion chamber only by hearsay. He does not read the
trial transcripts. He gets an order signed by a judge
to hold a prisoner, that is all.

Still, we should confront the jailer as part of the
corrupt system. We should insist that what he is doing
is wrong.

In any situation short of a mass holocaust, you

would not want to go that far down the line of authority of those who are participating in evil to those who, like the jailer, are very far removed from the actual killing.

But again, to understand it clearly, you have to understand the dual nature of a lot of rescue work. We are there to save babies, but if we fail, we are not apologetic. We were not just "making a statement"; we were being faithful to our brothers and sisters. There are categories that people already understand that do not fit our work. When people ask after a rescue whether we achieved our goal, it is hard to answer. Most of the babies usually die after we are removed. Not all of them, but most of them. Were we trying to save a few? Absolutely not—we were trying to save all the babies scheduled to die there that day. Well, then, does that mean we failed? No, because we were really trying to be obedient to the Lord, who asked us to rescue those babies. And if we were obedient, then the results are in God's hands, not ours.

But then as soon as you admit that your work might be valid even if it failed in its immediate practical goals, people say that you were just trying to "make a statement".

Fidelity is not a familiar category to most people. When you try to explain that you were simply being faithful to the Lord, to the Lord who said that when we serve our littlest brothers and sisters we are serving him, people do not understand that. It is an unfamiliar category.

And it is the same thing in trying to explain noncooperation in jail. We are not trying to punish the jailers. In fact, remember, most of the punishment that comes with noncooperation falls on the prisoner, not the guard. Noncooperation may have a practical effect, getting us out faster, and that is good. But it may not have a practical effect, and that is fine, too. If we suffer lovingly for the babies, that is a good thing.

It is funny how people forget that rescuers can get hurt in their work. Rescues, especially large rescues, can be very powerful. If you have enough people, the mill may simply close down. And then proabortion feminists scream, look at what those male chauvinist pigs did. But the point of a rescue is to be faithful to the babies, and sometimes you get hurt for that.

If you think of the rescues as an exercise of power, then maybe it is not good if the rescues are done by a lot of men. But when you understand that part of a rescue is taking responsibility for babies and taking risks to protect babies, then of course it is good that men do rescues.

There are different things you can expect in jail. I wrote to Joe Wall that he should not be upset about the shackles the guards put on me. When you are in a prison, you have to understand that the guards who are dealing with you have procedures designed for violent criminals. That is reasonable, since most of the prisoners are violent criminals. So the guards have to shackle them or risk their own lives and the lives of other people in the community if the prisoners escape.

I was shackled, and it was unjust. But I think you have to pick what you will complain about and let a lot of things go. The shackling was not a deliberate effort to break Joan Andrews; it was part of a policy that usually makes sense.

The guard may not even know who you are or what you might do to him. In that situation, you accept anything that happens to you, and you offer it to the Lord.

We have to try to find a balanced response to the things that are done to us. Some things that happen are totally unjust, like the torture that we see at the abortion mills sometimes. A police officer knows you are not going to attack him, but he tortures you to extract "compliance". "Compliance" sounds so nice and reasonable. But that is what torturers have always wanted: compliance.

Still, we should never complain and gripe about it. It is awful to hear prolifers griping about what the officers did. You have to say something to the officer when there is torture, asking him why he is doing that. We should intercede for each other. But griping is awful.

When we are trying to follow the Lord, he takes care of us. Nothing happens that the Lord does not see. If we offer him the gift of quiet endurance, he is pleased with that.

We are in God's hands, even when we are being dragged around. Sure, the police should not do it. But we should never forget that God has us in the palm of his hand more securely than the police ever will. And our response to him should always be full of gratitude. If God decides that we are worthy to share in the suffering of his Son, we should thank him, not complain.

There is always a balance to strike.

Joe Wall wants us to demand that we be treated as prisoners of conscience, not as regular criminals. That is a good idea, and with our growing numbers, we will get "POC" status. Then maybe we can get rid of the shackles. But in the meantime, the shackles are not that bad, and we should not complain about them.

We must not complain, but we do not have to co-operate, either. The shackles are part of a system. And we should decide not to cooperate with that system.

The prison guard is not as involved as the police officer, but he is a part of a system that has been corrupted. There is a mass holocaust going on, and it is not isolated to the one arena of the abortion mill where the killing actually takes place. That is just the apex of it. It is supported by the policemen who remove you, by the courts who sanction it and by the criminal justice system that incarcerates you or extracts a penalty when you are sentenced to do community service.

When you are ordered to serve the community, that is saying you did something wrong to the community, you did a disservice to the community, and now you have to do something good to counterbalance that. But the truth is, rescues do not harm the community.

When we are fined, the money goes to a corrupt system to help support the criminal justice system that does not protect the helpless, does not deter the killers and jails the rescuers.

When we are in prison, we cannot save babies directly. That is a serious wrong committed by the jail system. We should be able to protect our brothers and sisters, and anybody who stops us from that is doing wrong, regardless of their excuses.

Incarcerating a rescuer is "material cooperation" in the killing. If the rescuer were free, a life would probably be saved.

Rescuers aside, most prisons and jails cooperate with killing the babies in another way. They are accomplices to the holocaust in a very direct way. When a female inmate wants her baby killed, she gets all the help she wants. A woman loses all her rights when she goes to prison—she can't vote; she can't drive; she can't go out and get ice cream when she wants it; she can't call her family on the telephone when she wants to; she can't visit anyone when she wants to; she can't go out and see a movie. She loses all her rights—except when she wants to kill her baby. She has an absolute "right" to kill her baby, and the prison personnel will drive her to a mill as long as she pays for it. And in some states the penal system will pay for it. In Florida, she would have to pay for it herself. But once she has paid for it, she can have the abortion.

If her mother is to die, or her father dies, or her cousin dies, or her own child dies at home, there is no guarantee that she can go to the funeral. Most likely, she will not be allowed to go. She can beg to go, she can offer to pay a marshall to escort her to the funeral and back, she can go through all that rigmarole and paperwork—and probably she still will not go. She does not have that right.

But if she wants to kill her child, that is an absolute "right". That is first priority, top priority.

If that is not cooperating with the holocaust, I do not know what is. And how can you cooperate with a system that does that?

There is a massive holocaust in our land, and the

prisons are part of the system. The Supreme Court claims to have the ability to create or abolish human rights. Of course, they cannot do that; rights are given by the Creator, and they are inalienable. But people pretend that the Court has this magic power to wave a wand and make black into white, and white into black, to make crime a virtue and virtue a crime. Maybe tomorrow they will abolish the stars.

This insane claim to bogus authority is being accepted by the rest of the federal courts, who set aside state legislation intended to protect babies.

When rulers use the appearance of law to enforce their edicts, that is a tyranny. And the only way to stop a tyrannical rule, with its mass murder, is to refuse to cooperate in every little way that we can.

Noncooperation in jail is just one way to reject the tyrannical system. There are many other ways—for example, refusing to pay taxes to a government that kills babies.

Different people will find different ways not to cooperate. Noncooperation in jail was my choice, but it does not have to be the same for everyone.

We should never cooperate with evil, but we all do to some extent. That is part of what it means when the Pope says that abortion is a "social evil". But we should try to free ourselves from this evil.

It can even be put in legal terms. There is a massive effort to kill babies in this country. It involves the courts, the hospitals, the insurance system—all the major parts of our social fabric. This killing is often done with our tax dollars, and is always done with the tacit permission of this "tolerant" society. That could be described as a "conspiracy to commit murder".

If you are part of a group that plans murders, you do not have to be there on the day that someone pulls the trigger to be a part of the conspiracy. So we are all guilty of conspiracy to commit murder.

But there is a legal defense to the charge of conspiracy. If you make a reasonable effort to thwart that conspiracy, then you can be acquitted.

So you could say that we are all legally required to make a reasonable effort to thwart the American abortion system. There are many ways to do that.

In our lives, there should be a constant purging of all those little things in us that contribute to evil. We should always be trying to grow in holiness, in other words. That takes time, and the best way to do it is a question.

Ideally, no one should pay taxes as long as the killing is going on, and not only because some tax money is used for the killing of children directly. Even when the government is not paying the abortionists' salaries, it does allow abortions to go on. It is not that I do not love my country; it is that I believe that only if we stop this mass holocaust will our country survive. We are killing ourselves.

You have to do the best you can and be content with that. If you stopped buying products made by companies that support Planned Parenthood or some other part of the abortion industry, that would make grocery shopping a nightmare.

In many cities, when you throw out your trash, it is hauled off to a dump somewhere and thrown on top of thousands of little bodies that the abortionist tossed out last year. So you are desecrating the grave of a murdered baby. Does that mean that prolifers should devise an alternative trash service?

To be free of any taint of cooperation in abortion you would have to stop paying taxes, grow your own food and set up your own trash system, just for starters. That is what it means when there is a "social evil". We are all implicated; the society we live in kills babies. And even if somebody did withdraw from American abortionism, there would still be the problem that it is wrong to tolerate slaughter in your neighborhood. There are no innocent bystanders at the execution of the helpless. We are required to protect our little brothers and sisters as much as we can.

We are totally brutalizing our children, the ones that survive and are born. We are making monsters of them. I gave some talks recently in upstate New York, and the worst responses I had were at a Catholic school, talking to teenagers, who should be so idealistic. They were more negative than anyone else I had ever talked to. I talked about babies, and they insisted that I should not force my morality on someone else.

I had not expected that. I was just talking, as I normally do, about the little precious children, how they need protection and how brutal abortion is, but how we could convert minds and hearts by actually going out there and stopping the killing, and how mothers are so grateful after their children are saved, and no one ever regretted her baby being saved. My whole talk was about that. And the students wanted to defend the right of the abortionist to carry on his business, according to his conscience, his moral code.

Hitler had a conscience and a moral code. But his code was wrong.

There is an entire generation of kids who do not remember when babies were protected by law. For them, protecting babies is a weird new idea. By our slow, weak response, we have brutalized an entire generation.

It was hard to go to a Catholic school and listen to all this proabortion propaganda—"How can you tell someone else what to do with her own body?" The students have bought right into all the propaganda.

What can we do to reverse this total brutalization of our children? The only way they will ever see how horrible it is will be through our actions. They need to see that we are totally refusing to cooperate with it. They need to see that we refuse to bow down to the Supreme Court's tyranny, even when the authorities beat us up and drag us through the prison systems. Regardless of the risks, we will refuse to cooperate with the abortion holocaust; we will just sit there and say, "No. It's too ugly; it's too evil. We're not going to tolerate it. We're not going to support any aspect of it, no matter how distant from the actual moment of death, no matter how far down the road."

All the small assaults on the dignity of the babies add up. It is one pebble on top of another on top of another on top of another, until there is a huge wall, a massive structure of ignorance and hatred and death. Faced with that, we have to start undermining it to the best of our ability. We cannot totally eradicate it in one stroke, but we must keep trying.

The direct killing right at the abortion mill is clear. But the police who remove us, and then the court system that bows to a decision that is obviously null and void, the prison system that bars rescuers from saving babies—all those are very closely connected with the killing.

There are many other ways that we cooperate in the killing—by attitudes that we adopt or by the things that we tolerate and do not decry. All that contributes to the slaughter of babies. Even our language: we fall into saying that someone is going to "perform" a murder. You don't "perform" murder; you "commit" murder.

There are many small things that we do without thinking that contribute to the killing.

15 Following in Jägerstatter's Steps

By November 1986, I had been shipped to Broward and put in solitary confinement there for noncooperation.

While I was in solitary, I could still hear people in other cells and talk to them. And I went out in the yard for an hour a day, five days a week.

In the disciplinary unit, there were twenty to twenty-five cells, most of them double-bunk. There were a few people in protective custody, and they were not double-bunked. And I was in solitary confinement.

It was always overcrowded there. They had to build a whole new lockup unit there because it was the maximum security prison. They got the long-term prisoners, the lifers, but also anyone who could not get along or kept getting into violence at Lowell, the medium and minimum security prison. Like me, some people would go to Lowell for a while, but then when the system found them to be a big burden, they would get shipped to Broward. Then if people made trouble at Broward, they ended up in lockup. That was where I was.

There were frequent fights. Of course I did not intervene in all of them. For one thing, I couldn't, because I was locked up in solitary.

It was interesting when I did intervene. Most of the inmates will tell you to stay out of their fights. It is like the guard-dog mentality: if you go between a guard dog and the person the dog is attacking, the dog may go for you, even if you are its friend.

An inmate would say, "Look, I like you, and you've been nice to me, and we're friends—but don't you interfere in my business with somebody. If I have a fight, you stay out of it." Or they would tell me that if I got in the way, then I would be the one to get hurt.

But what happened most of the time was that they would be careful not to hurt me. They would punch around me, reach around me to grab the other person. Even while they were trying to kill the other person, they would not hurt me. They just looked at me.

They told me they would take me apart, and I was afraid they would sometimes, because people in there really got angry. "How dare you interfere!"

But they never went after me. In fact, they were protective of me, and when other inmates made remarks about me, they would explode, and then I would have to defuse that.

There were not a lot of fights about me. I was not a big topic or anything. But a lot of inmates liked me, because I was decent to them.

There was a lot of coming and going in lockup, and only a few inmates were in the disciplinary unit for long terms. They would be in and out in thirty or sixty or ninety days. I did about twenty months there.

It took a while for prolifers to figure out that a five-year sentence really meant a five-year sentence. There had been all kinds of threats for ten years. This sounded like a more serious threat. But even after I was sentenced, it took a while for people to catch on that it was for real.

After I was sentenced and shortly after I was moved south, there was a rally in Pensacola to show solidarity. In fact, that was the first time that Randy Terry from Project Life in Binghamton took a leadership role in the rescue movement. Randy was with us on the steps of the Supreme Court in 1985, when a group of us were arrested for praying to the wrong god at that temple, but in Pensacola he took a leadership role, working with John Ryan.

People went to the abortion mill and then to the judge's home. There were a few arrests at the mill. Some people came down to the jail where I had been held. I heard that that was a crazy scene, with snipers on the roof to hold off the prolifers in case they broke through the barbed-wire barriers and tried to storm the prison to free me or something.

One of the people who came to that rally in Pensacola was Peter Lennox, who had learned about it from Joe Scheidler's hot line in Chicago. When Peter became a committed Christian, he also became prolife. He was really burdened by the holocaust. Then he met Scheidler and got involved in picketing. At Thanksgiving he heard from Joe that there would be a march in Pensacola to support me, and he drove down with some Atlanta people and joined the rescue there. After he went home, he got in touch with Susan, and then they started working together.

Peter really got involved in publicizing what had happened in Florida. He wanted to make a videotape of what had happened and publicize it to get more people involved, especially pastors. He wanted people to push for my release. Peter took it upon himself to make sure that people across the country understood what was going on. He started writing me letters every day and praying for me. He told me what he was doing to publicize the case.

Susan decided that Peter could help me, and she told me to work with him. He is very brilliant, and he was ready to put his time and energy and his own money into the work.

Of course, I can trust Susan to make sure that my convictions are not violated by people acting in my name. I had just been burned working with a well-meaning person who did not pay much attention to the way I do things, and I wanted to make sure that no one else did something that would compromise my beliefs in any way.

I was going through a hard time in December, January and February, very aware of my many failings, feeling really bad, depressed, worthless. Despite feeling really down, I knew that Jesus forgave all of my sins and all things. Even so, it was just a dark, dark period. All the joy was gone, all the joy I had had up until then.

When I went to Broward, things got really bad. It was so brutal. There was homosexuality at Lowell, but it was much more intense at Broward. I saw things I still do not want to talk about. It really made me feel bad. I was overwhelmed by the constant evil and ugliness.

I had been in solitary confinement since I went to prison at Lowell, since I left Escambia county jail. I stayed at Escambia for a week after my sentencing, and then, on October 1, I was sent to Lowell. I had been in solitary since then, except for the first ten days at Broward.

During those ten days, I was in three different lock-up cells. Inmates kept getting into fights, and to break up the fights the guards would switch people around. But eventually my noncooperation landed me in solitary.

November, December and January were rough. The rest of that year was hard too, but it was most intense during those months.

I was grateful for Peter's letters. He was suffering, too. It took a long time for things to start getting better. But it was nice knowing that someone really cared. Peter cared about me, and he went to work to get me out.

He worked hard to let people know about my situation, and he was a great support in very bad times. He worked hard to distribute literature about the situation in Florida and urged people to write to Florida's governor, Bob Martinez.

After I had been in jail for a while, I started getting floods of mail. It poured in especially after Marlin Maddox, an evangelist with a nationwide radio program, talked about what had happened in Pensacola. He talked about it on two programs, and then later he kept referring to it.

Before that, I had a few good friends writing letters here and there. Once in a while a prolife newsletter would tell the story and that would bring in some mail, but it was manageable. After the Marlin Maddox show, a whole load came in, and the mail stayed heavy after that.

The people who wrote were outraged at the injustice of punishing someone for protecting little babies.

Many people said that they were concerned about the babies, that they were of one heart with me about that. Many of them said that they had never thought about getting out and doing something about it, and now they were. That was the best kind of comfort I could get, that people were going to do something. I was really touched by that.

As time went on and I got more publicity, I began to see that some people were looking at me as a hero. I felt really uncomfortable with that. Most people would say they were involved in rescues partly because I was in jail. It made me feel great that they were active at the killing centers, trying to stop abortion. But when they would explain that they thought I was some kind of hero, I felt they didn't understand. God put me in the position I was in, and his grace sustained me. But I was grateful for their loving, tender hearts.

I know how I feel about prolifers who get long sentences. I just love them so much, and it breaks my heart.

Since I got released, people have asked me to talk. I thought that would last for a couple of weeks and then calm down, but people kept asking. That still astounds me. But I am glad I can be used to get people out to do rescues. That pleases me. Wonderful people are listening and are starting to do rescues.

But some people put me on a pedestal. They do it out of the goodness of their hearts, but I do not belong there. We all have to be open to whatever God's will is, whatever might come in the future. We have to be totally committed, no matter what. Eventually, there are going to be people who get killed for protecting

Joan Andrews talking into a tape recorder during an interview at the Women's Correctional Institute, Claymont, Delaware, 1988.

babies. But we must try to do God's will, whatever that entails. That is the bottom line.

A generation from now, people will look back, and they will find it hard to understand why we thought some things were important. Ten years ago, people who went out and did some picketing were regarded as exceptionally dedicated. Of course they were dedicated, but why was it exceptional?

I have been to jail for a few years, and right now that seems exceptional. But in a few years, that will change.

Prolifers are trying to identify with babies who are being killed. The older babies, who are killed by late abortion, are tortured for hours before they are killed. So it is not really so exceptional when some adults go to jail for them. People who follow the Lord have always been willing to give their lives for others.

I did not do anything amazing or unusual. There were lots of people doing the same thing, and lots of people going to jail, but no one knew about them. It is just that people heard about me, and thought in their hearts that they too should be out there stopping the baby killing.

The volume of my mail did not mean much to anyone else in the prison. I was not notorious. For me personally, it was beautiful getting all these magnificent letters. In fact, it was overwhelming. Some inmates made jokes about it, but it did not really mean a whole lot to them.

When I began to get lots of stamps, that meant something to other inmates. They would come by my cell to get stamps. I gave away a lot of stamps. That was the one commodity I had. I did not have any personal clothes, but I had stamps. They would come by the cell, or I would go out in the yard and slip them stamps to write to their families. But then I realized that they were selling them for other things, so I stopped.

I decided I should just do my prolife work with the stamps. But for a long time I gave them out.

Peter Lennox worked hard to put pressure on the governor. I was definitely in favor of that; he should have been pressured. I did not know what would be the best route to take in order to get out, but that seemed reasonable, and it is good for rescuers to try to get out.

We are going to rescue babies, even if that means jail or death. And when we suffer for the Lord and his babies, that is an honor. Still, we have work to do outside jail; we belong outside jail. We should try to get out, without ever compromising.

At first, I was uncomfortable with the campaign to get me out. The focus seemed to be on poor Joan in jail, not on the babies who were dying. It took me a good year before I felt comfortable with the effort. I was penny-wise and pound-foolish at the time. My idea was that if a rescuer goes into jail, people should pay some attention to that and try to get him out, but the main focus should always be on continuing rescues. However, there is no conflict.

I was not smart enough to realize that a large rescue movement cannot be built that way. I began to realize that if we do not stand together in solidarity and get our people out of jail, then all the rescuers could be put in jail, and others could be scared away from rescues, and then the babies would not be protected. I realized that in the long run we have to work to get our people out, but without ever losing the focus on the babies. We have to get the rescuers out if possible, so that they can continue to protect the children.

I told Peter Lennox that whatever might be spoken of or planned, the babies come first. If a demonstration was planned to publicize my situation, it should include a rescue. In fact, the rescue had to be the main focus.

There was some talk of a sit-in in the governor's office. I did not oppose that idea as long as there was also a rescue at the death house and the rescue was primary.

It would have been unwise to let the state get away with the plan to crush rescues by putting all our leaders in jail or picking individuals at random and making examples of them. As time went on, I realized that I was being used to send a message of fear, that I was the one they had chosen to make an example of. It was a deliberate effort of the powers that be in Florida to crush rescues and scare everyone away from ever doing rescues. It had to be dealt with.

My decision about noncooperation came from that new understanding. In conscience, of course, I would never agree to cooperate with anything that would contribute to the death of a child. But Florida's effort to make an example of me and crush rescues added a new element. I decided that not to cooperate in response to their challenge was important, too, and worked in conjunction with the conscience imperative.

This new threat had to be dealt with, and firmly. It was not just me but also others at stake. So the Florida powers had to learn that when they tried to

Joe Wall and Joan Andrews, dancing, 1985.

Joan Andrews and Bishop Austin Vaughn (N.Y.) leaving courtroom, Dobbs Ferry, New York, 1988.

break us, there would be consequences for them. They had to learn that we would adopt a noncooperative mode of behavior, and we would never back down.

People outside the jail would focus on protecting babies, but they would never compromise those in jail and would keep up the pressure for justice until the system had to back off and release the rescuers.

In the fall of 1987 Joe Wall did me a tremendous favor. He is always watching out for people, and he has been a great friend for years. Long before he started doing rescues himself, he supported them, and educated people about them. But that fall, he recruited Richard Cowden-Guido to write about my situation.

Joe started sending Richard letters and articles, telling him what was happening in Florida. Richard was not opposed to rescues; he thought they were a good idea. But for him they were just one of the nice things to do. Of course, he thought it was too bad that this woman was in prison, but the world is full of problems. But when he sat down to read through the pile of letters and articles, he became convinced that rescues were the right thing to do, and that eventually he should be participating.

In November 1987 Operation Rescue had a preliminary rescue in Cherry Hill, New Jersey. Randy Terry had been recruiting for over a year for rescues to start in New York in the spring, but they had decided to have a trial run. They chose the Philadelphia area, because that was where the strongest rescue community was. Richard wrote to me before the Cherry Hill rescue to say that he was planning to go to that rescue. He said that once he had read all the letters that Joe sent him, he was committed to rescue. He had decided it was the right thing to do, and he was very happy about it.

The rescue went well. There were 210 people arrested there, with some people still blocking the door late in the afternoon when it became clear that there would be no killing there that day. It was a tremendous success. Finally, there were more people ready to risk arrest than in the rescue in Gaithersburg in 1984.

In that rescue, Randy Terry showed that he could bring out large numbers of people and maintain discipline. It was a very encouraging start.

After the Cherry Hill rescue, Richard decided to do a book about rescues and about me. He asked if I would give him permission to gather letters to and from me, and I agreed. He worked hard to get the book ready before Operation Rescue started in the spring, because he thought it would help in recruiting. In fact, he was the one who persuaded Bishop Austin Vaughan to join the rescue in New York.

16 Prayer in Solitary

The most painful part of being in prison was that I could not get to Mass. That may sound curious to some people. But I love Jesus, and he is present in the sacraments. His grace, his love, comes to us through the sacraments.

I was able to receive the sacrament of confession in prison. Sometimes it would be two or three weeks before I would be able to go to confession, although the priest there would try to make it every week. But still, it was very painful not being able to be present at the Holy Sacrifice of the Mass. That was rough—not just when I was going through a hard time in 1987, although it was especially hard then. It was rough for the whole time in Florida.

Before I went to jail, I went to Mass every day.

Imagine being cut off from a good friend, or your wife or husband or children. Imagine not being able to be with them, not being able to participate at the most important events of their lives, missing the wedding of a daughter or the baptism of a son. That was the way I felt about not being able to be at the Holy Sacrifice of the Mass. Jesus is there, and we are present at his act on Calvary, his brutal death. He died because he loved us. Imagine a friend, your closest friend, the person you love most in the world, being

217

brutally killed because he loves you. He is dying for you—and you cannot be there. It is painful.

I was able to read Scripture, and a priest did bring Communion. But still, nothing takes the place of the Mass. I cannot put it into words very well, but there is something about the Mass that you know and you feel: everything that is going on, the privilege of it, the honor of it, the beauty of it and the pain of it.

It is such a joy. It never gets old. Sometimes, being human, you might neglect to be aware at every Mass of just how tremendous it is, how awesome it is. But then when you shake yourself into awareness, you are just so awed and overwhelmed each and every time.

Imagine being deprived of Mass not only during the week but also on Sunday. Not just this week, but the next week also and the next week. Not just this month, but the next month also and the next. It was devastating.

At the same time, I realized that it was something that God was allowing.

One of the hard parts of it was that I knew it was in my control. I could go to Mass if I gave up my noncooperation with institutionalized evil.

Another time of pain was Friday evening and Saturday morning. I knew my friends were out there rescuing babies. There was work to be done, and I was not there to help.

In the midst of this holocaust, it seems that the only time you can feel good, feel relief, is when you are there blocking the killing. It is so sad when you think of the places where children are dying and no one, not a single person, is there. Children die without anyone caring or pleading on their behalf.

The hardest prolife work of all is sidewalk counseling. The community Catholics United for Life (CUL) in New Hope, Kentucky, has done so much to protect the babies and has been faithful for so long! They propagate sidewalk counseling. The hard part of this work is that when the mothers do not accept your help and they go in to have their babies killed, you stand there and pray for them, and you do not block them. You pray for them and get ready to try again when the next family crisis walks down the block. That is just the toughest job I can imagine.

The people who do sidewalk counseling do not burn out if they have a strong prayer life and a great peace and acceptance of God's will. They can see the merit and the necessity of being there to save the lives, working on behalf of the children and mothers. They do not burn out, but it is extremely painful.

When you block a door, it is a great feeling. Nobody dies while you are there. There is just no greater feeling; it is wonderful. There are different parts of that feeling. Most important, of course, is that the little children need you to be there, and you want to be there for them. But also, you love your fellow rescuers, and you know you are there with people who will take some risks to protect other people.

The feeling of solidarity is perhaps similar to what soldiers feel. So on Friday evenings and Saturday mornings, I felt the way soldiers might feel if a battle were going on and their buddies were on the front lines and they were somewhere behind the lines, in a hospital somewhere or—worst of all—on leave. You just want to be there, you want to be with your comrades, to help and protect them.

Broward was not a vacation, a period of rest and recreation. But my friends were continuing a struggle, and I was not with them.

When I was a little kid, I thought to myself that if my brothers went to war, I would have to pretend I was a boy and stow away on the ship, so I could protect my brothers, just be there and make sure they were okay.

Rescuers feel that way about each other. We want to be with each other to make sure no one gets stomped. Or if he does, you can be there with him and see if he is making out okay.

That feeling of solidarity is secondary, of course, to the commitment to protect babies and women from abortion. But it is still very strong. We are family. When my friends go on rescues or when they are on trial, I want to be with them.

Whenever I heard about a trial that was coming up, especially when I heard that there was not going to be solidarity and someone was being singled out, I would feel really frustrated. I wanted to be there to urge people to stand firm and protect one another.

The Pope, in his encyclical on labor, says that much of the dignity of a person is connected to the work that he does. Our work is not a punishment; it gives us much of our dignity.

My work is saving babies. People say of that that I am a professional trespasser or a professional protester. There is some truth to it. In spite of the scorn, the truth is that rescuing babies is my work. And it is a source of dignity. I miss my work when I cannot do it.

When I was at Lowell, on a team that was reviewing my case there was a counselor who was very scornful of rescues. She called John Burt a bum and criticized his maternity home. "He's freeloading on society. He lives on donations."

I said that was a wrong perspective. He was taking these women in who would otherwise be a burden on society. He took them in for free, shouldering that burden himself, then accepting donations from people who freely wanted to help. I told her he used his own home, and the foundation money was all his own. He poured his own money into it.

In the early days of this country, a teacher was paid with produce—eggs from one farmer, corn from another farmer, a day of plowing for his garden from a third. It was in payment for his teaching their kids. He was not freeloading; he was doing a service. He was taking care of the kids. John Burt was doing the same; he took care of those women, and that is a real service to society.

When we are out there protecting the children, we are doing a service, too.

I said that when I travel around, people give me money that I do not earn for what I do. The work of protecting babies has to be done, and everyone should be doing it. But a lot of prolifers who believe in the dignity of these children cannot do what I do. They want to protect the babies, but they have children of their own, maybe, or other responsibilities. So maybe they give me a little bit of money so I can travel around and do what they would like to do but cannot.

The counselor did not want to hear about it, though. I tried to explain it to her, but she just did not hear it.

Since I got out of prison, people have given me more money than they used to give. Before, I got just enough for bus fare once in a while. Now I get enough for plane fare.

Many of the prison officials were negative about what I was doing. I guess they felt I was undermining their work. If you are not cooperating, then you are saying something about what they are doing.

Some of the prison officials stood up for me, however. Once, I got in a discussion about Mary and about Medjugorje. I mentioned that I thought that our Lady might be appearing in Medjugorje, and I was telling this to some southern Baptists. One woman said, "That's fanatical! I know a Catholic man. I asked him about it, and he said there's no such thing going on."

I said, "Well, no, Catholics do not have to believe in it."

But she went on and on. I kept saying you do not have to believe in it. I said that the Church has not made a pronouncement on Medjugorje. None of us is supposed to get too attached to anything we hear about before the Church offers some guidance. But we can still listen to the renewed call for prayer and fasting. Those are good in and of themselves, and they do not contradict any Catholic teaching. And I said that even with those apparitions that have been approved by the Church, we are not required to believe in them to be Catholic.

Still she went on and on about her friend.

Finally, another official piped up and reminded her, "She just said you don't have to believe in it to be a

Catholic. So this neighbor of yours evidently doesn't believe it. That's okay."

I was glad he stuck up for me. I had kept saying the same thing, but the woman just would not hear me.

I said the Rosary in jail a lot. It is a beautiful and powerful prayer, and I just love it. It gives me great solace.

Jesus gave us his Mother to console us, to be close to us, to pray for us, to lead us closer to him.

I feel very close to Mary. I love her, and I would pray the Rosary because she asks us to pray the Rosary. She asked not only at Fatima but also at Medjugorje. And she asked us to do a little fasting, to do penance. In doing these things and in trying in some way to do acts of reparation for the sin of abortion and other sins, praying for the conversion of individual souls and our country and the world, I feel a great peace.

I also prayed some devotional prayers and the Divine Office. I probably was not doing the Divine Office right, not following the right readings for the day. I was all mixed up. I had one volume of the Office that was just for one season, instead of the four volumes, so I just kept saying it. It has some beautiful prayers at the back, too, that I loved reading.

First I had the volume for the Christmas season. But when I was transferred to the state prison, I was not able to take that with me. Later, when I was in Delaware, I got the Easter volume, and then I had that one for months and months.

So I said morning prayer, evening prayer and night prayer for Christmas and Easter. It was good.

Through Mary, I am able to feel the gentleness of

God, because God was so gentle in giving us his Mother. He knew we needed to feel that feminine love, the gentleness of a woman. So he gave us his own Mother. When he spoke to John from the Cross, he was speaking to us also.

There are some people who did not have a loving and gentle mother. I do not know if they could understand Mary. I would hope they could. I cannot imagine how someone would not.

I felt, and I feel, such love for our Lady. I ask her to pray for me and to stay close to me and those whom I love, showing them her maternal love for these children. It helps me, consoles me, when I am feeling frustrated or when I am hurting in any way.

When I feel I have sinned—when I know I have sinned—and when I want to straighten out my life, I feel so frustrated. There were times in prison when I was thinking about all kinds of weird ways to escape, all kinds of crazy things. It is hard to maintain perspective when you are trying something new and there is no one to talk to about it. You make mistakes and think about even worse mistakes. I got close to some crazy decisions. I needed Mary to be with me. I needed to be close to our Lady. I needed that contact.

When we are struggling to separate out our imagination from real contact with Jesus Christ, there are Scripture and the Tradition of the Church to help us. We can separate what we imagine from what is real and solid and clear. But what we know with clarity and certainty about Mary is very limited.

Still, the little we know is so rich. She was invited by the Father to be the Mother of Jesus. That shows a great deal about God's respect for motherhood and invites us to think about her.

She lived with Jesus for years, and he submitted to her. He listened to her when he was deciding what he would do. That is astounding. She was with him when he started his ministry, and she stayed with him throughout. She was there when he died. In fact, her fidelity to him when he was crucified is the best example for explaining what we do at rescues. Peter wanted to use violence, and when the Lord said not to do that, he did not know what to do and ran away. But Mary was just faithful, present. There is no clearer explanation of prolife nonviolence than her example.

Mary was there when Christ rose. She was there with the disciples, praying, when the Holy Spirit descended on them.

Even if you just set aside the idea that we might be able to know something about her, it is still a very good idea to try to imagine what her life would have been like. At Pentecost, was it familiar for her, or all new? Or both?

But I believe that the Tradition of the Church does help us to know her. Through the traditions—not only of the apparitions but also of the devotions to Mary— we are invited to learn about the Lord through her.

Mary has a mother's heart, and she loves the priesthood of her Son Jesus Christ. Priests are very special to her. They need special prayers, and they need special love from us. Things like that are affirmed for us through the Tradition of the Church.

I needed contact with Mary when I was considering ways to escape and going through other times of severe stress. There were times when I felt so unworthy, but

I knew she was there with me, helping me pray, praying for me.

Bill Hickey from San Diego wrote me a letter in which he said that he knew how much Mary loves me. He said he could picture her putting her arm around me and hugging me. I just started to sob. He built such a beautiful picture. He was making up the picture, but not the love that she offers. It was Bill's picture, but *her* love.

I knew Mary, and she did love me.

God loves me, and of course I know that. But emotionally, I needed a mother's love. God gave it to me through my mother when I was growing up and through Mary when I was in prison.

I remember sitting on the floor of my cell and just sobbing when I read Bill's letter. I do not cry very often, but that really hit and made me feel good. I had been praying the Rosary every day, many, many times, but I did not realize that deep down I was not feeling Mary's closeness because of my own feelings of not being worthy. The prison system gets so bad. I knew Mary was faithful. I knew the Lord was with me there. But when Bill wrote that, the way he pictured her love for me, it just broke my heart.

17 Freedom!

In December 1987, I was moved up to Delaware. The governor was under pressure to do something about me and decided at least to get me out of the state. The decision to move me was described as a humanitarian gesture, since it put me closer to my sisters in Delaware and Maryland, but that was probably not the whole truth.

I did not hear about the move until the week before Christmas. It came as a big surprise.

I got a call from Tom Bush, a good lawyer who had been working to help me. He said that they were going to be transferring me because they wanted to get rid of me. He explained that Governor Martinez would say it was to put me closer to my family. And he said that Delaware had agreed to accept me. He wanted to know if I would agree to go. I said I would not agree to do anything, but that they could do whatever they wanted with me. But in my heart, I was thrilled.

Around noon on Christmas Eve, some guards told me to pack up. I asked them where I was going. They did not tell me, but I knew anyway.

I packed. That was the only time I packed up; all the other times, I had been totally noncooperative. I did not have any clothing, because I had donated my clothing when I first got there. All I had was two boxes of letters.

They took the boxes, but then nothing happened. Finally, they said, "Never mind, you're not going." And that was it.

But on Christmas morning, around 4:00 A.M., some officers came for me and told me to go with them. They took me out in a small car, and they drove me up to Florida's medium-security prison at Lowell and dropped me off there around noontime. I spent the rest of Christmas day there.

The next morning, I was taken by van with two officers all the way to the federal prison at Alderson, West Virginia. I spent a month there.

Most of the prison at Alderson looks like a college campus, with red-brick buildings, tree-lined streets, a pretty field and gigantic hills all around. Most of the inmates cannot even see any fencing. There is a low fence around the perimeter of Alderson, but I could not even see it from where I was. The only place that looked like a prison was my building, the confinement unit, with the tall fences and razor wire. It is a white building, and they call it the White House. "You're going to the White House", they said when someone got in trouble.

I had a really big window, and I could see the other inmates as they walked through the compound to work and wherever they were going during the day.

On New Year's Eve, the guards and inmates had a bonfire on the other side of the field. It was beautiful. They sang carols, but it was too far away to hear clearly. I could hear that there was music but could not follow the words.

There had been a bonfire on Christmas Eve, and Squeaky Fromme, who had tried to shoot the President, ran away that night. She did not get far before she was found and captured. No one escaped on New Year's Eve.

After about a month, on January 22, they finally got around to moving me the rest of the way. I did not know when they were going to take me, and then all of a sudden they came that morning and took me.

It was great. I had thought I was going to be stuck at Alderson forever.

I asked my transportation officers if they would take me by Washington and drop me off by an abortion mill for a couple of hours. I knew that my friends were rescuing babies somewhere there that day. Later, I learned that there had been a rescue at New Summit abortion mill. Christy Anne Collins went to jail for five months for that rescue; they isolated her and made an example of her. But when she got out, she kept rescuing babies.

But that day, as we got near Washington, my guards said we could not stop, because we were going the long way around the city, not into the city at all. They drove me up to Claymont, Delaware.

Claymont was very overcrowded, of course. There were people sleeping in the hallways, on the floors of the halls and on the couches in the general recreation room. People were stuffed into cells, sometimes four people to a cell. That meant that some people were on a tiny space on the floor with their heads right by the toilet. And our toilets sprayed. The poor person on the floor at any given time would get sprayed when anybody flushed. It was sad.

The tensions were high. Summer would have been miserable. I had been there in the summer in 1985 for forty-two days, and there was no air conditioning; it was just sizzling hot. But this was overcrowded and tense and cool.

Delaware has only one prison for women. If a woman is arrested anywhere in the state, she may be in a little holding tank overnight at the police station, but then she is sent to Claymont. So in one wing were people doing life, and in the other wing were "detentioners", people who were just awaiting trial.

There were different-color uniforms. If you wore brown, you had been sentenced. If you wore green, you were waiting for trial or sentencing.

Of course, I had been sentenced, but I was given a green uniform. I stayed with the detentioners. It was like being in disciplinary confinement, because the detentioners are locked down over twenty hours of the day.

When we did get out, we walked the halls and walked in the tiny little recreation room. There was no gym, of course, even though there were people in there for life. But it was sad: when you walked the halls, you were told to sit down. One officer who was almost always on duty, a lieutenant, would say, "I'm going to lock you down in your cell if you don't sit down." So you sat in your cell all day and then came out to sit in the halls.

During rec, the two hour-and-a-half periods we had each day, if we walked the halls at all, we had to watch out for the lieutenant. We would get up and walk across the room and sit down together, then walk across the room to talk to someone else. We had to play different games.

During the spring and summer, inmates would be allowed outside. Around Eastertime, they finally would begin to get out, maybe once a week for an hour, at one of the recs.

There was a tiny little inner court area with a volleyball net. The lifers got out a little bit.

The nice thing about it was that I was with other inmates. We would pray together. In fact, there is still a group that started when I was there that prays the Rosary all the time.

A couple of the women were Catholic, or fallen-away Catholics, actually. But they came back to the Church. My friend Father McFadden, a rescuer from Philadelphia, came to say Mass once a month. A few prisoners came to Mass, then more and more. And some women started taking instructions to become Catholics. Some of the Protestants prayed with us, including the Rosary. We would get five to seven people every day. That was great.

The atmosphere at Claymont was not brutal. But the guards were tough. If someone got out of line, they beat her up. But then they were friends again. It was different from Broward, where there was so much hatred and where the violence was so much more intense and threatening.

There was a lot of homosexuality, of course, as in every prison. It was not as visible, but it went on at a very high level in the prison.

Homosexuality was much more visible and vocal and violent in Broward, where it was constant. It was in every other word from almost every inmate. In

Delaware, it was just as constant, but much more low-key, less expressed, less visible. Still, it was very much there.

The guards were involved, too, and there were favors and so on. That corruption went quite high up, and it was common knowledge who got what favors and why.

Still, Claymont seems to have some scraps of the spirit of the woman who ran it twenty years ago. She was the first warden. She treated the girls as if they were her daughters who maybe had gone a little bit awry. And she had meetings with them, and the doors to the cells were always open. It was not locked down then. She was like their mother, and it was wonderful. The girls really responded. The doors were never locked unless someone really got out of hand, and then when someone was locked down, it was usually not even for twenty-four hours. The girls would really try to behave, because they loved her. The prison was run like a home, not like a state prison, and it went beautifully. She died, and the place has changed, but the lifers and the warden try to help maintain a halfway decent atmosphere. The prison's history did have an influence on them.

In mid-February I finally got to Mass for the first time since June 1986. It was tremendous. I was on a high the whole time I was in Delaware, because I was able to attend Mass every month.

Father McFadden was a rescue priest, a prolifer. He wore the "Precious Feet" pin, showing what baby feet look like at ten weeks, when most abortions are done. And he talked to the girls about rescues. He mentioned that he had been in jail briefly and said that the short period he was in gave him a little taste for what they felt. He really related to them, and they loved him.

The first Mass I attended, they just brought up a few Catholics and a few others we encouraged to go. There were maybe ten of us in all.

There was a nun who would come out once a week and have a Communion service. But some of the Catholics there had not been to Mass for years. They almost never had Mass there.

Right after his first Mass at Claymont, Father McFadden said that even after I left, whatever happened to me, he would still come out to say Mass for the women once a month.

So the Mass grew and grew. As people heard about it, more and more came. Eventually they had to have it in the mess hall, because the whole prison showed up. By the time I left, the whole prison was showing up for every Mass.

Father McFadden showed a film on Medjugorje. It was great. People wanted to have Rosaries and read the Bible.

In most prisons there is no Catholic outreach. Maybe there will be Mass once a week, but then all during the week Catholics are abandoned. There are good Christian groups who come and evangelize, with prayer groups. They reach out, urge others to come to Jesus, to give their lives to God. But you never see any Catholic outreach.

But at Claymont there was a Catholic revival, because of that rescue priest. You know how they are: they want to save everybody, not just the babies.

While I was there, Bishop Robert Mulvee of Wilmington said Mass at the prison. Every year, around Easter, the bishop says Mass at a prison. One year he will go to the men's prison down in Smyrna, and the next year he will go to Claymont.

After Mass, Father Clement Lemon introduced me to the bishop. Father Lemon had been pastor in Newark, Delaware, when I lived there with Susan.

I saw Father Cusack, my spiritual director, every week. He was away all of February, but I saw him at the end of January, and then every week from March until June. This meant more to me than I could ever relate.

There was a prison official named Vincent Ryan who was very upset about that, and he thought I should not be allowed to see a visitor because I was not cooperating. Why should I get the privilege of seeing a spiritual director when I was not cooperating? He tried to stop it, and he actually brought it up at a prison board meeting. My visits were cut back to a short time, and there was some concern that they would be cut off altogether. But shortly thereafter I was moved back to Florida anyway.

My noncooperation caused a big uproar at first at Claymont, and the guards kept me locked down for a couple of weeks. I would not stand for count. All the prisoners had to come out of their cells and stand for count, but I would not do it.

After a while, the guards just ignored it.

But in May, I said that on the first of June I would extend my noncooperation. I would leave the cell any time it was open. At meals, you are supposed to go out and get your tray and come back in. I said I would go out and not come back in. I would go out for rec but would not come back in. I would go out for a shower but not come back in myself. Every time the door was open, I was going to do whatever I wanted to do. I would be as big a burden as I could be. If ordered back into the cell or to do anything, I would just sit down and be limp. Full noncompliance.

I wrote to the attorney general of Delaware, and I told him that I had been treated very kindly but that if Delaware was not able to release me I should be returned to Florida. If they kept me in custody, they would be cooperating with Florida in my incarceration.

I knew they did not want to hold me; the attorney general had written a very strong letter to the Florida officials, criticizing them publicly. I knew they thought they were doing me a favor, because I was close to my family, able to see them. I had phone privileges; they never took that away, even though I was not cooperating. So it was a nice prison. But if they held me, that would be wrong, because no state should cooperate with the injustice of another state in holding a rescuer, preventing a rescuer from protecting children.

So I said that I would start a new policy on June 1. I would totally refuse to cooperate with them, the same as I had in Florida. That was more trouble than the Delaware prison could handle, so they sent me back to Florida after a couple of weeks.

I told them I regretted doing it, and I really respected everything they had done. But I said that it was a matter of principle. There was a degree of complicity. Florida should not think that they could wash their hands of me and let someone else do all the dirty work. If they wanted me in custody, they would have to do it themselves. They should not think that any other state was going to cooperate with them in this.

Beginning June 1, I was kept locked in all the time. Anytime the door was open, I would squeeze out. They tried to keep the door open, with a guard standing right there blocking it. But as soon as the guard walked away, I walked out, and then they had to drag me back in.

At first some of the guards got really upset with me, because they had been treating me really nicely. But eventually they started laughing about it. We would joke about it. But after two weeks, they came for me, and shipped me back south.

They took me to Alderson again for one night. The next day, we drove to Lowell. I arrived late at night at Lowell, almost midnight. The next day they took me to Broward.

I did not get there until late afternoon. They took me to the back gate, and we sat there in a van for a long time, because the guards were busy inside and could not come out for us. Then they got a wheelchair, because they did not want to carry me or drag me through the whole compound.

The warden wanted to talk to me for a few minutes, so I was wheeled into her office. I told her that I would not cooperate with anything until I was released.

Then the guards took me to process me into the prison. They wanted to search me, but they knew I had been in custody. They knew I had been strip-searched at Lowell and everywhere. They knew they did not have to do it. And they had quit searching me before I left Broward six months before.

But state officials in Tallahassee had been saying openly that they had ways to make me cooperate. When people called Jim Smith, the Secretary of State, he made ominous remarks about "breaking" me. He said that they would make me cooperate.

So they pushed ahead with a brutal strip search, including a search of all my bodily cavities, a more invasive search than I had ever undergone before. It was like a rape. Six women and one man stripped me and pried everywhere.

I had been a little apprehensive about what was going to happen, because normally I would have been wheeled right into the lockup, because I had been in custody and they had quit strip-searching me. When they brought me up there for a strip search, I told them I would not cooperate. I would not strike at them, but I would hold onto my clothes. They said that meant that a male officer would be used.

I said that in conscience I could not go along with this any longer. It was not necessary. It was immoral. They stripped people to dehumanize them. I told them that if they tried, I would hurt myself.

The male officer got some scissors and tried to cut off my uniform. Then he started ripping it off. I slipped to the floor and started banging my head. I had told him at the beginning that if they forced me, I would hurt myself. Later, they said I was hysterical, but I was not. I had told them very calmly what I would do, and I did it.

I had been forcibly stripped before, at Alderson and

in Pensacola. But this was the first time that they had brought in a man.

In Pensacola, I held onto my clothes, and they hand-cuffed me to the bars. But there it was still all women who searched me. Women can do it; women are strong enough to subdue a prisoner. They are trained correctional officers, and they can get the job done.

I was not violent. I told them that I was not going to touch any of them, but I was going to hold onto my clothes. With a male officer there, I held on tighter and twisted more. I guess it did take five of them.

They never told me who gave the orders for the strip search. I saw the warden and brought it up. She said she had her orders from Tallahassee.

At one point, I took out my eye—the prosthesis—and threw it across the floor. I thought that if they saw that, maybe they would be horrified and feel they were going too far, and maybe they would quit. But it did not work. They were tough—who cares about an eye?

They knew I was not smuggling in drugs or weapons. It was like their exams for VD; they knew I was a virgin. But they used the excuse of "normal procedures" to strip me, and then went way beyond that to humiliate me.

Then they took me back to the disciplinary unit where I had been before Christmas.

At that point, I refused all comfort. I would not accept the sheets when the cell opened for me; I scooted everything out. That night, when I was sitting down thinking about things, I thought about the children, how they are deprived of all comforts. I decided to refuse everything, even showers, from then on. I would keep one set of clothing, but nothing else. That evening, I also damaged my prosthesis. I remember thinking that it would be a visible sign of my commitment, like bruises all over my face. I wanted them to see that I meant it when I said that if they stripped me, I would hurt myself.

When they were holding me and stripping me, I could not bang my head. I said, "Okay, you can hold me, but you can't watch me for the next four years. And every time you strip-search me, I will hurt myself."

Sitting there in the cell, I wondered what I could do without really hurting myself. The prosthesis was already damaged. I knew I would have some painful repercussions from that, because putting something rough in the eye cavity is very irritating. So I just scratched it up, made it all rough.

I am not going to say that that was a good idea. Maybe I made a mistake. But before you judge, think about the situation. Jim Smith was saying openly that they were going to break me, and my introduction to the new policy was like a rape. I could not ask anyone for advice. And I was determined that I would not hurt anyone else.

The whole idea of nonviolence is to deflect the violence of some social injustice toward yourself and absorb it and forgive. Violence can go on and on forever, until someone breaks the cycle by forgiving an unjust assault.

Looking back, I can say that absorbing violence is one thing and inflicting it on myself—for whatever reason—is another. But that was what I did.

The next few months were dreary. I had cut off all communication, except for emergencies. I refused to talk to lawyers (except for the last couple of weeks, when John Broderick got involved). But it made me feel close to the babies. I was really devastated about the strip search, but at the same time I felt closer to the children.

I had a Bible and my Rosary and some devotional things I brought back with me. I was allowed to keep those.

I wrote only rarely. Before, I would spend most of my day in writing and prayer, but mainly writing. But after returning to Broward, I spent most of my time praying, all day and most of the night.

It was hard to sleep at night, because it was cold and damp, so I would sleep maybe for about four hours; then I would wake up, and I would pace my cell to get warm and then lie right down. My days and nights were filled with prayer. The Lord pulled me through that time.

I was known as "the crazy lady". Prisoners would tell each other: "She's the crazy lady. She blew up an abortion clinic, you know. She never takes a shower. She doesn't sleep on her mattress; she's on the floor under her bunk. She's crazy."

Newcomers on the unit would ask, "What's that old lady doing here?"

And someone would say, "She's that crazy lady."

"Oh, that explains it", the newcomer would respond.

After a while, some of the people who knew me from before got sent back into the disciplinary unit for different things. It was good to hear them defending me: "Oh, no, that's Joan Andrews. She's sweet."

The old-timers were a real boost. "Joan, how are you doing? Want to pray? Let's pray together."

When I first went into confinement in 1986, there were constant hostility and anger, and there was incessant homosexual behavior, with inmates attacking both guards and each other. When anyone came in the unit, there would be whistling and comments about the women, but never about the men, because it was all homosexual. It was incredible.

But when anybody started talking about the Lord, the atmosphere changed. After we had been praying together for a while, many of the girls would say good night to each other, and then they would say, "God bless you; good night. I'll pray for you, and God bless you."

There was hardly a night that went by without some sexual encounter in the cells around me. I heard some pretty bad stuff going on. But sometimes, after the uproar, I would hear them say to each other, "Okay, now you sleep well; God bless you."

I am sure the Lord has a beautiful heart for them. They are just so brutalized. They grew up using people and being used, and that is all they know. That is why they love prolifers and other people who are there because of the Lord. They realize that we really care about them and really love them.

I am not a warm, outgoing person like some people. Some prolifers go to jail for a couple of days and they just talk to all the inmates and get to know everybody. I am not that type of person. I really hold back. I am embarrassed and self-conscious and self-centered. If somebody talked to me, I would respond quietly. But eventually even that would touch them, because they are so starved for honest love.

They know when you genuinely care about them and are praying for them. They know you love the Lord.

They called me their friend, and they really protected me. When guards said something nasty to me, a couple of them would say, "Okay, we'll get her", or, "We're going to beat her up."

Then I would have to say, "No, no, don't do that. She's under pressure herself. She has orders."

Once a month, when the prison would order me to cooperate, and I would refuse to cooperate again, and they would keep me in lockup for another month, the other inmates would support me. "How can they do that to you? You never do anything wrong, and they keep you in confinement. They're harassing you."

Some of the officers were supportive. They were sweet and apologetic: "I'm sorry to have to do this. I know you cannot cooperate. But I have been ordered to ask you, to order you back in."

Others would just be nasty about it. Then the inmates would start yelling, "Why don't you leave her alone? She never does anything wrong." God bless them. They figured that I was a good prisoner because I was kind of quiet all the time.

At the end of September, I got an urgent message from Susan to call her. The only time I would take calls was when it was an emergency. I did not know if she was calling about a death in the family or what.

Susan said that a lawyer named John Broderick was coming down to see me and that I should listen to him, because he had her support. I should do whatever I could with him.

I agreed to see him. At first I was not hopeful about it, because he did not understand rescues at all. But after two days, we began to make some progress. We worked out certain absolutes that he would not transgress. And he said he would get me out.

Basically, the Florida authorities wanted to get rid of me, but they felt they needed to save face. So John was going to try to get me extradited. He wanted me to agree to be extradited.

I said, "No way; I'm not cooperating at all."

John explained that they wanted to give me clemency, but I would have to agree to be extradited, so they could save face. I said no.

He got all upset with that. But they had to accept it. Finally they extradited me anyway. The final stroke that broke the Florida resolve to hold me the full five years was the huge Tallahassee Freedom March, rescue, and take-over of government offices by prolifers in August 1988.

They had to bring me into court forcibly. On Friday, October 14, they brought me into court in Miami, where a judge identified me and agreed to send me to Pennsylvania for sentencing there in a Pittsburgh case dating from May 1985.

The extradition hearing was in Miami. I drove in with the warden, Maria Villacorta, and a guard. The court complex in Miami was huge. In back of the courthouse was the county jail, connected by a walkway. A guard told me that almost eight hundred prisoners a day go into court, back and forth to court from that jail.

When we drove into Miami, the warden said, "Boy, I never had treatment like this." The police at the courthouse stopped the traffic for us when we came in and out. They were expecting us, and we went right in.

Joan Andrews' return to Pittsburgh from Florida. Joan being led through airport terminal by deputies.

The warden drove in and parked, and they closed the gates behind us. We went up to the courtroom, and there were reporters there. The judge let them film the whole thing for television, right inside the room where the meeting was. He looked like William F. Buckley.

I did not cooperate at all. The judge said, "This is October 14. And you are Joan Andrews." I did not say anything.

He said, "I think you are Joan Andrews. I've got your picture on my desk and the statement of these officers that you're Joan Andrews." I just kind of smiled.

And he said, "Okay, you are Joan Andrews." Then he looked at the warrant from Pittsburgh and said, "This is a valid warrant. You are Joan Andrews. So I rule that we will extradite you."

He was really nice about it. I would not cooperate, but I was hoping he would extradite me. Then he said, "Have a nice trip", and that was it.

Then they signed some papers, and I was sent back to the prison.

When we left, the guards ushered us to the warden's car and opened the gate, and again some officers went out into the street to stop the traffic and stood there while we drove out. It was different.

When we got back, a girl who was in confinement—in protective custody, because her life had been threatened—called to me. She said, "I just heard over the radio that Martinez has signed your clemency papers!" She said that they would not go into effect until I was sentenced in Pittsburgh. She had all the details. So I knew that I would be transported pretty soon.

I did not know when I was extradited that the clemency would really happen. They could have sent me off to be sentenced in Pennsylvania just to get rid of me, and then let me be held in Pennsylvania under their sentence. I still had over two years left in my sentence.

I did not know what the decision was until I heard about it from the radio report. It was a big relief. Oh, it was glorious!

On Sunday, two marshalls from Pittsburgh came. There was no strip search; they just patted me down. Then they took me on a plane into Pittsburgh. I was there for a few days, until Tuesday, the eighteenth. Then they let me go.

In Pittsburgh, I went before ex-Jesuit Judge Raymond Novak again. He had locked Joe Wall and me up for a couple of months already. He gave me three years' probation. I told him I would not accept probation, but he said he was not asking me whether I accepted it; he was just imposing it.

I was released from prison without signing a thing. I just walked out.

18 The Harvest Is Rich

The day I was released from prison, I went to Mass
with my friends to thank God for his love for all his
children. Since then, I have been running around giving these miserable talks that people are very kind
about. I have been doing some rescues.

It has been very encouraging to see that rescues
have grown so much, and I am very grateful to Randy
Terry for his love of the Lord and love of babies and
mothers.

Ten days after my release, I attended a conference
in Toronto sponsored by Human Life International.
There was a rescue there with enough people to shut
the mill for the day.

At a rescue in Connecticut, I was very surprised to
see how many people had grown into a commitment
to solidarity with the babies and with each other. Even
lawyers were talking about solidarity.

I joined "Rachel's Rescue" in Washington, organized
by Kathy Kelly, Kathie O'Keefe, and other women
who have had abortions. I know that I will learn from
them more about the rich reward of sorrow, the joy
of knowing God's healing love.

Father Norm Weslin has started a group of rescuers
who will identify with the babies by taking the name
"Baby Doe" and will be noncooperative, doing penance

for the evil of abortion. I hope to work with them as much as possible.

I expect to concentrate on a rescue outreach group, sending people overseas to start rescues in other countries. In many countries, abortion is still illegal, but babies get killed anyway. Planned Parenthood says the thing to do about illegal abortion and all the complications it causes is to legalize it. I say the thing to do about abortion, whether illegal or pseudo-legal, is to stop it.

We will teach people how to do rescues with clear ideals and principles of rescue, with everything centered on prayer.

The day I was released, the first reading at Mass was from the Second Letter of Paul to Timothy:

> At the first hearing of my case in court, no one took my part. In fact everyone abandoned me. . . .
> But the Lord stood by my side and gave me strength, so that through me the preaching task might be completed and all the nations might hear the gospel.

The second reading for the day was from the Gospel according to Saint Luke, who loved Mary so much and wrote about her and whose feast day it was:

> The Lord appointed a further seventy-two and sent them in pairs before him to every town and place he intended to visit. He said to them: "The harvest is rich but the workers are few; therefore ask the harvest-master to send workers to his harvest. Be on your way, and remember: I am sending

Joan Andrews, Albin Rhomberg and John Cavanaugh-O'Keefe at Morgantaler's abortion clinic in Toronto ten days after Joan's release from prison.

Joan Andrews and her nephew Michael Brindle.

you as lambs in the midst of wolves. Do not carry a walking staff or traveling bag; wear no sandals and greet no one along the way. On entering any house, first say, 'Peace to this house.' If there is a peaceable man there, your peace will rest on him; if not, it will come back to you. Stay in the one house eating and drinking what they have, for the laborer is worth his wage. Do not move from house to house.

"Into whatever city you go, after they welcome you, eat what they set before you, and cure the sick there. Say to them, 'The reign of God is at hand.'"

Praise to you, Lord Jesus Christ.

Photographic Credits